Learning Journalism Where Writers Rise
Four Enlightening Years in Graduate School at the University of Illinois Urbana-Champaign

Sal Nudo

Table of Contents

.

Dedicated to my wife, Jill, and podcaster Rob Dial.

Acknowledgements

I would like to thank the following scholar-practitioners for contributing their thoughts and knowledge to this book: Leon Dash, Matt Ehrlich, Brant Houston, Rich Martin, and Jean McDonald.

I would also like to thank Jessica Elliott, Janelle O'Dea, and Teryn Payne, three former students who were in a few of my graduate classes and have gone on to pursue careers as a postsecondary educator, a journalist, and a communications professional, respectively. These women were kind enough to reach back into their minds to recall course content and relate their thoughts on classes that occurred several years ago. It was fun catching up.

It's hard to believe that when I started this book, I had no intention of interviewing other people. When I reached chapter three, however, it became apparent that the thoughts of my former professors were required to make this book complete. Along with answering my questions, Professor Leon Dash was nice enough to give me access to Room 336 at Gregory Hall—during COVID-19 when classes weren't happening on campus—allowing me to see that personally revered space again and take pictures for description purposes in this book. My chat with Dash was followed by interviews with some of my other former journalism teachers. They made this book far richer with their wisdom and further helped me explore a topic I care about. It was wonderful to see their faces and hear their voices again, even if it was via Zoom most of the time.

Author's Note

A big reason I wrote this book was to relate the values and practices of journalism for aspiring journalists, and for those who simply have an interest in the field. While the time-honored principles of journalism haven't changed, and shouldn't, there is no doubt that the business models of newspapers and the practice of reporting are constantly in flux and evolving. Some of the material in this book relates the state of certain aspects of journalism from several years ago. That doesn't mean readers won't learn something from this information, or that it is not still relevant. On the contrary, these portions of the book may provide useful snapshots of where journalism was not all that long ago, and what it can be going forward.

"Think through what you've got."
- The only line of notetaking from one of my
Literary Feature Writing
classes on April 13, 2016.

.

Intro to Journalism

Nearly ten years later, the receipt is worn and faded. Actually, it was a washed-out piece of paper the minute the cashier at the Illini Union Bookstore handed it to me—the printer must have been low on ink. A decade of passed time has not improved the look of this rumpled, five-and-a-half-inch receipt. Despite the lightness of the black ink, I can still see the staggering cost of the textbook: $93.10. The "10" in the price is faint, almost completely faded out.

August 31, 2012. The date of the purchase of my first textbook in the master's journalism program I was about to embark on. The title of the book, *Mass Media Research: An Introduction* (I purchased the ninth edition), now sounds more enticing than the content inside of the book turned out to be. On this day, though, it didn't matter. I wasn't in the mood to read much of anything, which is saying a lot considering how much I love reading.

I exited IUB and dragged myself back to my parked car, the campus sidewalks teeming with University of Illinois Urbana-Champaign students, most of them years younger than me, their demeanors coming off as overly chipper with the new semester underway. It was 5:30 p.m.—I know because of the time stamped on the receipt—and gray outside, cloudy.

Ten days earlier my wife, Jill, experienced a miscarriage, losing the only spawning of human life she and I would ever conceive. I was still numb and despondent over the incident, wondering if a guy on the verge of 40 had any business undertaking the pursuit of a master's degree—in journalism, no less. As much as I revered the field, it was an undeniably dying one. A second postsecondary degree could help me in my job as a communications professional, but did I have the energy to pursue such an endeavor?

It was hard to fathom that a little more than a month ago—July 24, to be exact—my world had been rocked with the news that I would be a father. Jill had texted me a photo of the pregnancy test she'd taken showing a large + symbol, as an IT guy was fixing the computer in my office at the Alice Campbell Alumni Center, where I worked. I could barely contain my euphoria—I seriously wanted to announce the news to the IT guy—and rushed down the stairs to call Jill outside the building. We were both giddy with excitement and, frankly, surprised it had happened after we'd all but given up on conceiving. Weirdly, as I was talking to Jill, I remember a girl in a bikini was chatting about something with a cop in the parking lot. You remember these details when over-the-moon news suddenly hits, or at least I do.

Earlier that day I'd received an email that revealed a decision had been made as to whether I'd been accepted into graduate school. After logging into my university account, I read the first paragraph of a letter:

Dear Salvatore:
We are pleased to inform you that you have been admitted to the Graduate College as a Journalism program student for the Fall 2012 semester. This letter is your official notice of admission.

Yes, it's fair to say that July 24, 2012, was a happy day for me, perhaps the happiest of my life. And the news about being accepted into graduate school accounted for only about

10 percent of what made that day so special. The other 90 percent of my happiness was, of course, due to the baby we were having.

But our child wasn't to be. The night of Jill's miscarriage, I went to bed early and turned out the light of our upstairs bedroom, alone. The window was open, and a shining full moon was high overhead, directly in front of me. I looked up to it, crying. I think I may have prayed. The sadness was overwhelming, perhaps the most intense grief I had ever felt to that point. But if there was a beacon of hopefulness, it was this: Prior to that moment, I didn't know I could hold so much love inside of myself. If our child had been born—and believe me, I'd thought a lot about what our lives were going to be like after he or she was—I would have done anything in the world for that little human.

The answer to the question turned out to be yes—I *did* have the energy to pursue graduate school and never worked so hard for anything in my life. As down as I was on that late-August day exiting the campus bookstore, I was taking a step toward something new and unknown, a path of study and practice that would lift me up.

The following four years turned out to be some of the best ones of my life.

Master of Science Degree in Journalism Graduate Courses

To graduate from the news-editorial sequence with a master's degree in journalism, a student must meet the general University and College requirements for the degree and must complete 32 hours, which are composed of the following courses. A typical sequence would be as follows:

JOUR 400 Reporting 1 (4 hours)
Fundamentals of journalistic writing; reporting news of public affairs.

JOUR 425 Graphics and Design (4 hours)
Principles of visual reporting and editing. Introduction to newspaper page design, information graphics research and design, photojournalism, online design, and project planning.

JOUR 505 Master's Proseminar (4 hours)
Introduction to scholarship and research in journalism and mass communication examining theoretical approaches to the meanings, uses, and effects of mass media in society; discussion of media freedom and accountability; humanistic and social scientific contributions to understanding mass communication.

JOUR 415 Reporting 2 (4 hours)
Study and extensive practice of in-depth public affairs reporting – its concept, techniques, traditions, ethics, and social obligations.

JOUR 420 News Editing (4 hours)
Newspaper editing and headline writing, news judgment, ethics, and leadership.

JOUR 500 Issues in Journalism (4 hours)
Seminar on issues of contemporary importance in journalism in their historical, multicultural contexts. Emphasis on ethical, legal, social, professional aspects of those issues. Aimed at helping students to develop their own journalism philosophies and high standards of conduct.

Electives
JOUR 482 Immersion Journalism (4 hours)
JOUR 452 Great Books of Journalism (3 hours)

Master's Project
JOUR 481 Literary Feature Writing (4 hours)
JOUR 515 Master's Project (4 hours)

The degree requires a minimum of 32 graduate hours, at least 12 of which must be at the 500-level, including:

A professional concentration of 16 graduate hours approved by the department. Candidates without undergraduate work in Journalism or equivalent professional experience are required to complete either the standard news-editorial sequence or the standard broadcast journalism sequence.

Eight or nine additional graduate hours total in Master's Pro-seminar (four hours), Issues in Journalism (two hours), and Special Topics: Readings (two or three hours).

Four graduate hours in thesis or preparation and completion of an in-depth professional journalism project.

At least three graduate hours in additional elective courses.

A graduate-level grade-point average of not less than 2.875.

Chapter 1: The Basics and Dignity of Journalism

In an age when journalism can often be agenda- and clickbait-driven, locally depleted, and, sadly, carelessly covered or just plain fake, it is informative and refreshing to come back to the first-edition book by Rich Martin titled *Living Journalism: Principles & Practices for an Essential Profession*, which I read early on in graduate school.

Martin was a hardworking journalist for thirty-two years. He cares about journalism and the morality of budding reporters who practice the qualities of truthfulness, accuracy, and humanity in their reporting. Martin's writing in his first-edition 2011 book ranges from humorously presented reminders on the basics of journalism to hardened admonitions to take things seriously and get the facts right in articles—every time. This advice may sound obvious, but journalists must have the rudimentary principles in mind when writing stories. Publishing correct facts and including at least two opposing viewpoints of an issue within an article are standard operating procedure for journalists who want to be trusted and successful in their work.

Though the black ink of newspapers courses through Martin's blood, the profession wasn't a foregone conclusion in his life. In truth, he sort of stumbled into journalism more out of desperation to find a job after earning a master's degree in English at the University of North Carolina at Chapel Hill. Martin got his start at his hometown newspaper, *The Gwinnett Daily News*, after writing a police brief based on facts he'd been given. He made the "agonizing" article deadline but was personally not impressed with his work. Nonetheless, he was offered a job as a reporter and took it. Many years later, when I interviewed him via Zoom, Martin told me: "I've gone back and read stories that I did, you know, 45 years ago, and they're pretty bad. There's some really bad stuff there."

Martin's humility is a characteristic he discusses at length in *Living Journalism*. Journalists sometimes get things wrong—it's an unfortunate part of the job. The important thing going forward is to learn from those mistakes and avoid them again as best as possible. Other aspects of humility in journalism include not making assumptions about anything, listening to interviewees with the utmost attention, and treating the subjects of stories with respect.

Early on in my graduate program, I did a profile piece on a person who was (and still is) in a same-sex relationship. I brought up the relationship status of this person during the interview because I thought it was an important aspect of the article. It wasn't. At the end of the interview, I was asked by this person to not mention the relationship in the write-up; the couple wanted to keep that information private. I agreed without argument and felt a little shamed for having brought up the topic in the first place.

A more seasoned journalist may have pressed the issue, perhaps trying to change the person's mind. Maybe some reporters would have gone off record to learn more about the relationship. But I could tell this was a sensitive area, so I respected the person's wishes. It would have been a different thing entirely if their relationship had been pertinent to the story I was writing, but it wasn't. So, it wasn't mentioned. My first encounter with humility in journalism.

Martin stuck with the journalism track as a young man, learning under the tutelage of a grizzled newspaperman named Billy Williams, who, Martin said in the preface of his book, probably didn't even realize he was acting in a mentorship role. "The best journalists care about the nurturing of new journalists," Martin wrote, perhaps explaining why he later got into teaching.

I met Rich Martin in 2007 or 2008, when I was first considering pursuing a graduate degree in journalism at the University of Illinois Urbana-Champaign. He was the first person in the department I ever talked to, and I was immediately put at ease by his folksy charm and easy-bantering demeanor. At the time, Martin was a professor in the Department of Journalism and director of the graduate program. He had dark, closely cropped hair and glasses and was dapperly dressed in a sports jacket and dress pants. I'm not sure if he was wearing a bow tie when I met him, but that was an ever-present appendage to his wardrobe, adding to his quaintness.

I imagine many of Martin's interviewees over the years were taken in like me by his even-keeled nature. He eventually became a managing editor during his journalism career and had to deal with frantic early-morning calls, personnel issues, and budgetary decisions. These were realms of journalism that may have had less appeal to him.

I'll always be grateful to Martin for reintroducing himself to me prior to the lecture section of the second class I took within my course requirements, Reporting I (JOUR 400). I was nervous about the class, and Martin put me at ease before it got started. As time went on, I really began to respect the combination of Martin's nice-guy sensibilities and past dogged tenaciousness as a journalist and editor. He was an outstanding instructor and likely influenced many aspiring reporters. The essays I had to write for the final exam in his class were the most intense few hours I've ever experienced in a classroom—my right hand was sore for hours afterward. But I also felt satisfied, like I was well on the way toward truly learning journalism.

Martin said that his final exam evolved over the years and was designed to evaluate what his students had learned about the broad concepts of the craft he practiced for three decades. Accuracy, skepticism but not cynicism, the basics of a story, and a journalist's curious nature were some of the topics he brought up during our chat.

"This is what the First Amendment does for us as journalists," he said at one point.

Numerous other recommendations abound from Martin in *Living Journalism*. If you want to be a journalist, he writes, it pays to be curious, skeptical, and determined. He also says to never overlook society's forgotten people or sectors. Be a watchdog at all times. These teachings can't be said enough to those who want to cover news for a living.

Living Journalism has a modern, on-the-spot feel. Mixed with journalism's time-honored guidelines and values, the book includes recommendations to live and breathe the credos of the craft Martin cares so deeply about. Yet the word "Living" in the book's title also indicates an ever-changing fluidity within media. Reporters should prepare themselves for an unpredictable occupation but never forget the basic tenets of journalism. From tips on how journalists should function during a sudden crisis to the all-too-common misspelling of names, *Living Journalism* offers plenty of on-the-job examples from experienced reporters who share what they have learned. The title of Martin's book influenced how I chose to name the book you are now reading ("Living Journalism" and "Learning Journalism").

Martin now lives in Virginia with his wife. He told me during our interview that a second edition of *Living Journalism* had just been released. In what must have felt like a full-circle moment for the now-retired Martin, he told me that much of the new material for the revised book came from fifteen of his former students who were practicing journalism. Some of these individuals he'd taught in his first class at Illinois in 2005, and others were in his classes

13

during the end of his tenure as a professor at Illinois. The former students he included in his book offered a wealth of varied experiences and observations, he said.

Like any field journalism has evolved, but the practices related in *Living Journalism* should never change. These sentiments by Martin in the second edition of his book caught my eye and nicely sum up what my former teacher was trying to do when writing *Living Journalism*: "Some of the values and attitudes may seem old-fashioned to you, but that doesn't mean they are outdated. They continue to apply to a journalism that is alive and essential today, and they are what journalism needs to remain vital and important to American society, and to the world."

Martin recommends reporters always stay curious and admit when they make errors. They should ask the right questions, listen closely to their subjects, be skeptical of the information they receive, and delve into their stories with gusto to capture all sides of the topic. And while centering attention on the underserved individuals in society in a watchdog fashion, journalists should also, according to Martin, practice compassion. This is one of the most memorable lessons I learned from him, and one that journalists would do well to take heed of today.

One of Martin's assignments involved critiquing newspaper articles that showed examples of solid, questionable, and poor journalistic practices. I selected a piece by three contributing writers of one article who displayed worthy reporting skills by exercising restraint and showing humanity after the tragedy of two deaths. Another journalist in a second article could have used better judgment in describing the scene of a fire where children were involved. Finally, the reporter in the last article did not, in my judgement, include a key part of an event in her story and neglected to get a separate viewpoint that was needed for balance. She also included a quote that defined the story, without pursuing the other side of the issue. What follows are the three articles I selected and my critiques of them, examples of newsworthy events that were reported in different ways and with different levels of ethics and expertise by the journalists who covered them. The headlines are shown as they were written in their publications.

2 killed in fire saved elderly woman

This article in the Chicago Tribune *related how two men died in a fire at a high-rise condominium in Chicago. Before dying of carbon monoxide intoxication due to smoke inhalation, however, Jameel Johnson, 36, and John Fasula, 50, worked together to save the life of an 81-year-old woman who lived on the seventh floor. It's both a heroic and tragic piece.*

The actions of Johnson and Fasula, as related in the article, were straightforward but monumental. Johnson worked for a cable company and Fasula was a maintenance manager for the Chicago Transit Authority. The men rescued the unnamed woman from her apartment and carried her to the elevator, where she descended to the lobby. Johnson and Fasula then grabbed fire extinguishers from the walls of the hallway and attempted to put out the blaze. Sadly, they were unsuccessful in escaping, and their bodies were found outside of the woman's condo.

To their credit, the writers did not make this an unnecessarily gruesome article. Instead, the three co-writing reporters of the piece described a scene that involved fire, carbon monoxide, and two deceased victims in a professional, respectful way. They conveyed the admirable actions of Johnson and Fasula aptly and attained meaningful quotes from the victims' relatives and friends, which provided readers with a genuine sense of who these men were.

Additionally, instead of including sensationalistic quotes that may have been available from eyewitnesses at the scene, the writers chose heartwarming words that respected the victims. The account of the fire was described in a detailed way, yet it did not contain graphic images that may have offended the family members of the two victims or the family of the 81-year-old woman.

Two recommendations in the Society of Professional Journalists' Code of Ethics are to "show good taste" and "avoid pandering to lurid curiosity." The writers of this article practiced those values. In chapters 13 and 14 of Living Journalism, *Rich Martin says journalists should be factual but always show empathy and compassion toward the people they write about. The article by this trio of* Chicago Tribune *writers demonstrated these journalistic values.*

3 children hospitalized after fire

The writer of another article about the scene of a fire did not demonstrate such prudence.

"Remember Your Humanity" is the title of Chapter 14 in Living Journalism. *Within the section, Rich Martin relates how important it is for journalists to treat their subjects with compassion. The way a particularly tragic story is presented, and the details within it, should have an empathetic feel, according to Martin, or some readers may be offended.*

It could be argued that journalists should put these values into practice even more when writing about children. In a short piece in the Chicago Tribune, *one writer did not practice these principles perhaps as much as he could have. The scene involved another fire at the residence of a family living in the South Side of Chicago. A 4-year-old child was described by the writer as being "critically injured" in the fire, while her two older siblings were said to be in good condition.*

A neighbor named Sandra Gray, who lived in the unit below where the fire occurred, heard her 16-year-old neighbor screaming for help. The Chicago Tribune *reporter wrote a convoluted paragraph in which succeeding events are hard to follow, culminating to a quote that reads:*

"The 10-year-old ran back there to tell her (their sister) was on fire," Gray said. "She came downstairs and was knocking on everyone's door. She was screaming, 'My sister's on fire.'"

This quote is redundant and too evocative. The writer could have paraphrased this account and worded it in a more respectful way.

The reporter ended the article by relating how the 16-year-old burned her hands while trying to pick up her severely burned sister, an overly vivid detail that could have been left out.

This was a short article with newsworthy punch, but the telling of it was not as sensitive toward the family of the 4-year-old girl as it could have been. Writing in a dignified way about someone who goes through a traumatic event is a news value shared by Martin in Living Journalism *and in the Society of Professional Journalists' Code of Ethics. It's a principle journalists should adhere to.*

SEIU Local 73 members picket heading into strike authorization vote

At approximately 4 p.m. on January 23, 2013, several members of the Service Employees International Union Local 73 on the University of Illinois campus gathered in front of the Alice Campbell Alumni Center on Lincoln Avenue. It started as a small gathering but quickly grew, and by 4:15 there were approximately 40 people picketing to raise public awareness of the group's contract negotiations with the U of I. The scene was highly visible from my office window that overlooked the area.

The picketing was at first nothing out of the ordinary as protests go, but the group was vocal. Loud chants and noisemaking items were prevalent as the SEIU members formed into a narrow oval on the sidewalk and walked. One of the group's leaders stood atop a low wall in front of the half-circle drive of the building, megaphone in hand, leading the chants. At some point he stepped down from the wall to respond to a reporter's questions.

At approximately 4:45, the group moved toward the building's front entrance. At first it appeared that the SEIU members and other protest participants, who may have been nonmembers, were going to end their demonstration and would soon disperse.

Instead, most of the individuals walked into the Alumni Center, where they carried on with their picketing at full volume, noisemakers in full effect. This occurred on the first floor of a publicly used building where various events regularly take place and numerous Alumni Association employees work. The building's general manger had a short conversation with the man who had the megaphone outside, and the police arrived approximately 10 minutes after the SEIU members walked into the Alumni Center.

Following the arrival of the police, the SEIU members dispersed peacefully. The megaphone operator again talked to a reporter.

The next day, a reporter from The Daily Illini *wrote a short article about the event, which ran on the newspaper's front page. Halfway through the piece, a U of I building-service worker who partook in the demonstration said he was pleased with the turnout and enthusiasm of the picketers, as well as with the people in passing cars on Lincoln Avenue who honked in support of the cause. He then added, "The Alumni Center calling the police on us, it goes to reinforce the belief that a point has been made very loudly."*

This wasn't an inherently bad quote to include in the piece. Indeed, it shows the protesters were adamant about their demands and willing to have the cops called on them in support of their beliefs. The problem, however, was that the reporter failed to mention in the article the disturbance the picketers caused within a working environment indoors and the apparent illegality of their act. Without that information, the piece came off as one-sided in support of the protestors. The Daily Illini *article failed to include a key part of the story— the viewpoints of the cop, the general manager of the building, or even Alumni Center employees who were working at the time. Adding the thoughts of any of these individuals would have rounded out the story much better and made it a more thought-provoking article.*

Chapter 8 in Living Journalism *relates how crucial it is for journalists to get close to the stories they cover. To the credit of* The Daily Illini *writer, she was physically at the event she was covering. Unfortunately, she did not take full advantage of that fact. Perhaps she left the scene early or felt the last part of the demonstration that took place within the Alumni Center was not newsworthy. Perhaps she was biased in favor of the protestors. Whatever the case, her "antennae" was not fully up and attuned to her surroundings, as is recommended in* Living Journalism. *As someone who witnessed this event from start to finish, I felt the writer's story was incomplete. Attaining the viewpoints of all involved parties is a recommended practice in Chapter 13 of* Living Journalism, *and again, it's a practice that can't be preached enough to aspiring journalist.*

This protest right in front of my office was a lucky break for me as I was searching for something to write about for Martin's assignment. I'm glad I was attuned enough to see that a news story was unfolding right in front of me that day. The resulting critique of *The Daily Illini* article captures an interesting scenario and highlights one-sided journalism. It was satisfying to be a part of an on-the-spot event that allowed me to evaluate a subsequent article as I was learning about the golden rules of journalism.

The second part of the Reporting I class was a "lab" portion taught by Jean McDonald, whose journalism career included working in varied roles for more than thirty years at *The News-Gazette*, the local newspaper in Champaign-Urbana. McDonald made my pursuit of journalism feel like a less intimidating endeavor. She was knowledgeable, open, and entertaining. One time in class she mentioned how much she loved the show *Downton Abbey*. Not long after, the show became the first one—of many—that my wife and I binge-watched together.

When I talked to her by phone in 2021, McDonald related to me the universal elements of journalism such as dealing with words and language and possessing curiosity and questions that inevitably come to the fore in life.

"I think it's not rocket science, in that anybody should be able to learn how to do it to a certain degree," she said. "After that, you have people who do it much better than others."

One day in class McDonald related a story about a writer at *The News-Gazette* whose article was not up to par, and how she handled the situation as editor of the sports department. For this particular story, the N-G writer and a photographer traveled to East St. Louis, which, at the time, was a prime area for discovering potential Illini football recruits. While there, the writer visited players' homes, talked to football coaches, and stopped by a playground. Upon his return to Champaign, he was excited to write the story.

When McDonald edited the piece, she used a particular color of highlighter to highlight all the quotes in the story; then, using a different-colored highlighter, she highlighted what the writer wrote beyond the quotes he gathered. She discovered it was about an even breakdown and told the writer, "You could have done this story by phone."

McDonald was perplexed because the writer had returned from East St. Louis with interesting factoids for the piece. For instance, he'd walked across the blacktop of a playground and had heard glass crunching under his feet; another time, a coach apologized to him about the nasty smell in his office—a rat had died behind the wall.

"Those are sensory things that obviously he noticed, but they weren't in the story, and they helped tell the story," McDonald said.

Though the journalist was "ticked," according to McDonald, he eventually saw his editor's point and rewrote the article, which turned out to be leagues better than the initial effort, McDonald said. Her point to the class was that every writer needs an editor, no matter how difficult it may be to hear feedback. Sometimes the critique reveals small mistakes, and sometimes the advice leads to redoing everything.

"If you go into journalism with an ego, you have a problem," McDonald said. "Of course, there's all sorts of stories about journalists with huge egos, but you have to have the knowledge to know it's okay to ask for help. And you have to know that everybody's going to read your stuff, and why would you not want it to be as good as it could possibly be?"

I could have used that advice about a year earlier, when I traveled to Chicago to write an article about the Chicago Blackhawks' team doctor named Michael A. Terry. The piece I turned in to *Illinois Alumni* magazine wasn't bad, but I regret not taking better advantage of being in the presence of Terry, in his working environment in Chicago. Closer observations and a more in-depth interview would have revealed the many details that were right in front of my face.

In my article, for instance, I didn't convey Terry's harried manner during his busy work schedule that day at Northwestern University Feinberg School of Medicine, or even what he was doing. I failed to mention his tousled brown hair and friendly, accommodating demeanor, little but noteworthy particulars that would have given readers a better sense of his looks and personality. As busy as he was, Terry mentioned we could go to lunch and talk more extensively following our initial interview, yet I didn't take him up on that. I regret not capturing the many interesting things that I, as well as *Illinois Alumni* readers, missed out on by my not having lunch with this doctor, who probably had loads of great NHL stories to tell. What I submitted to the magazine was a by-the-numbers piece that could have been written by doing a phone interview with Terry, no different than what *The News-Gazette* sportswriter had initially turned in. It was a lesson well learned, one that McDonald aptly conveyed to our class.

Another lesson I learned in McDonald's class was the importance of collaborating. One of our hands-on assignments in the course involved teaming up with a few classmates to scout an area in Champaign-Urbana and coming up with a story. This, McDonald said, was how real-world journalists found great stories. They get curious about things and ask citizens questions. They talk to people and utilize social media to see what the masses are discussing. They look at press releases and read everything in sight.

"If you get a journalism job somewhere, you're going to be put into a situation you don't know anything about," McDonald said. "Ninety-five percent of the time, especially when you're starting out, you're going to be in a community you didn't live in. You're not going to know anything about the town. You have to be observant, you have to check things out, and give a fresh eye sometimes."

I look back on this assignment with both fondness and regret. One of the partners who worked with me on this community-centered journalism project was Teryn Payne, who is now the director of strategic communications & logistics for Chance the Rapper. At the time of our collaboration, she was an undergraduate who would go on to earn a bachelor's degree and a master's degree in journalism at Illinois. Her love of writing, photography, and page design pushed her toward the journalism field.

Myself, Teryn, and another classmate named Abhijit hopped into my car and headed to the spread-out vicinity of southeast Urbana, where we were told to go. The three of us simply walked around the area looking for and talking to everyday individuals who might provide us with an interesting story. I recall chatting with a few people in front of their apartments and talking with the proprietor of a business that sold food. Some firemen in the vicinity also gave us their time, and I remember thinking that writing about their occupation held lots of potential.

But those recollections of our visit to this area in Urbana are far from complete in terms of what we came up with for story ideas. In a late-March memo I sent to McDonald, we presented her with ten topics that included talking to individuals who had to deal with leaving a condemned apartment building; delving into the possibility of a bike path for residents in the area; and contacting the local public bus service about not running buses in the area enough, according to a resident we spoke with. Surprisingly, the story we ended up doing was the last one on the list.

In December of 2021, I reconnected with Payne via Zoom. Of the several individuals I talked to on Zoom for this book, the background behind Payne on my computer was by far the most stimulating. The large window of her high-rise home revealed a crystal-clear blue sky and the skyscrapers of Chicago's South Loop. As we chatted, I observed several times the small white sliver of an object floating in the sky behind her. I silently wished the planes Godspeed.

Payne has had a successful career in journalism since graduating from Illinois, having written numerous pieces for *Ebony*, *Jet*, and *Teen Vogue* magazines. In her super-busy job managing Chance the Rapper, whom she met years ago at a summer camp, Payne travels often and is in constant communication with many people. Our journalism project from 2013 was a modest start to her eventual careers in writing and communications, fields in which she has interviewed and dealt with many types of personalities.

"Believe it or not," Payne informed me, "as a child I was very shy. I feel like us having to go in the community and get out of our comfort zone and talk to people that we did not know—that helped me be more comfortable just interviewing whoever."

On that day in southeast Urbana, near the intersections of Philo Road and Silver Street, myself, Teryn, and Abhijit eventually made our way to St. Matthew Lutheran Church, where we met Pastor Robert Rasmus, a pleasant guy who agreed to be interviewed for our article, though the interview didn't occur that day. Our later talk with Rasmus took place on April 4, 2013, a date etched in my memory because it was the day Roger Ebert, who was born in and grew up in Urbana, passed away. I'd heard the news prior to meeting Pastor Rasmus at his church and was crushed. The longtime journalist and movie critic was a legend where we lived, and the way he had carried himself when his health began failing was every bit as inspiring as his rise from Urbana to the national spotlight.

When we arrived at the church for the interview, the pastor told us about his exciting background as a congressional press secretary and about his past career as a journalist. Incredibly, I didn't include any of this information in the article, which was more focused on the issue of crime in the area and how Rasmus's church dealt with it. Years later, I read a much better piece about Pastor Rasmus in *The News-Gazette* and was remiss that I didn't say one word in my article about his life prior to becoming a pastor.

Notice that I wrote "my article" to describe this endeavor. That's because, though this was a collaborative project in McDonald's class, I was the one who wrote the piece, without much help from Teryn and Abhijit. That was a mistake. The article would have been richer with their input and writing—I'm sure of it. In talking to Payne about this issue years later—and how bad I felt about it—she told me there may have been some blame to go around.

"You were older than us," she said. "Because of your maturity and experience with, not even just journalism but just working with other people, it was natural for you to want to take the lead on things."

Teryn said her mindset about college would likely be different now, as a twenty-eight-year-old, compared to how she was as an undergraduate student. Undoubtedly, she and I were in different stages of our lives when taking McDonald's class. Though this wasn't an excuse to avoid collaboration, it does reveal where our heads were at the time.

"I feel like I wasn't as focused, so not to put everything on you, taking some accountability on my end, I probably was slacking a little bit or made it easier for you to just say, 'Okay, I'm going to do that,'" Teryn said. "And I didn't give you any pushback because, you know, I was in college. I was living the life. I had just joined a sorority. I was doing so many things at the time."

I think McDonald suspected I had solely written the piece, because she pointed out the importance of collaboration after we presented our project in front of the class. These days I see prominent publications regularly using multiple writers in one article, and I wish I would have taken advantage of working with Teryn and Abhijit so I would have had that experience. Unfortunately, I was so focused on getting the story done, thinking I was the only one within our group who could capably write it, that I forged ahead on my own, writing an average article that could have been much better with my peers' help.

Here's the hindsight twist, however, and an example of how people can't always trust their memory as years go by: After talking to Teryn, I searched my Gmail account and was pleasantly surprised to find emails related to the project the three of us had worked on. Three of the emails included audio files I had sent to Teryn, since she couldn't be present for the interview with Pastor Rasmus. Here's what a following email from me to Teryn and Abhijit said:

Teryn and Abhijit,

I hope you both don't mind, but I wrote out a draft of our neighborhood story for you both to review before class on Tuesday. I figured starting the story now and checking it over would be MUCH easier than starting from scratch in class. Read it over and let me know if you have any suggestions. Here are some things I wanted to mention:

1) We need to have a little copy about a resident and a quote from a resident. Do either of you have a quote and description of a resident that we interviewed that you can email me?

2) Check out the headline and see what you think. Maybe one of you has something better.

3) I left a space in the story for info that may come from Diane Marlin, the Urbana city councilwoman for this area.

Teryn, I hope you got my transcriptions via email okay. If you didn't or if there are any problems, let me know and I can email you the Word docs with the transcriptions. I didn't copy everything word for word, but the important info is definitely there.

Thanks,

Abhijit wrote back saying "great story" and provided a quote. In all, there are numerous back-and-forth emails among the three of us centering on our project, one of which included Teryn relating how she could help with photos for the story. Another interesting tidbit to cap off our collaboration was that Abhijit reached out to Teryn on Facebook, around the same time I contacted her in 2021, for assistance on a research project *he* was working on.

So, after all these years, I discovered our three-person collaboration was more interactive than what I remembered, and it turned out to be a long-lasting partnership.

Another article I wrote in McDonald's class, "Cholesterol's debated role in heart disease," was nearly 2,500-words and included the insights of Illinois scholar Fred Kummerow, who is now deceased. The former professor is remembered as a cutting-edge biochemist and food scientist at the university. He was 98 years old when I interviewed him at his Urbana home.

On the back cover of his 2008 book, *Cholesterol Won't Kill You But Trans Fat Could*, Kummerow wrote that cholesterol is a "life-sustaining substance that has been unfairly implicated in heart disease." In the book, Kummerow said the standards of healthy cholesterol levels, as gauged by the American Heart Association, were not accurate, and that the focus on HDL (good cholesterol) and LDL (bad cholesterol) were overemphasized and incorrect. The right amount of cholesterol in an individual's body, he believed, was what's required to maintain good health—and everybody's body is different.

During his career, Kummerow analyzed the results of many blood plasma samples and arteries, consistently observing that people with both low and high cholesterol levels die of heart disease. His research covered the composition, structure, and biochemistry of coronary arteries, and what he found was that smoking, vegetable oils, partially hydrogenated fats, and fried foods should be avoided.

I enthusiastically absorbed this non-mainstream health information and was also thrilled to have landed an interview with documentarian Tom Naughton, a graduate of Illinois State University, for the piece. Naughton created the 2009 documentary *Fat Head* as a rejoinder to the movie *Supersize Me*, which he said "annoyed" him and is filled with caloric intake numbers by film creator Morgan Spurlock that don't add up. To prove his point that cholesterol was a "hugely important substance in your body," Naughton began to research health more intently and changed his diet to mostly include unprocessed whole foods such as meat, eggs, seafood, fruits, vegetables, nuts, and a little "full-fat dairy." The dietary changes worked for Naughton, who was fifty-four years old at the time. He said he felt healthier, slimmer, and stronger than twenty years ago. On his new diet, Naughton said he overcame asthma, psoriasis, arthritis, and rarely got infections.

To balance the article, I included the thoughts of the mother of my brother-in-law, Geraldine Wirth, who has since passed away but was at the time an advanced-practice registered nurse at the Decatur Community Based Outpatient Clinic, a satellite clinic of the Veterans Affairs Illiana Health Care System in Danville. Wirth conveyed both the benefits and harmful side effects of using statins to fight high cholesterol. I also talked to Paul Logan, a well-informed patient who had had his share of health problems and ups and downs with taking statins.

Finally, I interviewed and included the thoughts of Dr. Janet Brill, author of the book *Cholesterol Down: Ten Simple Steps to Lower Your Cholesterol in Four Weeks – Without Prescription Drugs*. This to me felt like real reporting. Talking to experts and getting their thoughts on topics they cared about; covering subjects I was interested in; and absorbing valuable information in a course I loved. I was only two classes into the program and had a long way to go, but it felt like pursuing a master's degree in journalism was a good decision.

Martin and McDonald were outstanding teachers who got me excited about journalism. They invited to their classes fantastic Illinois alumni who had graduated with journalism degrees and were doing exciting things in the field, relating their work to inspire me and my classmates. I think of these guest lecturers now and wonder if they're still working in journalism, especially given how battered the field has become, for various reasons.

McDonald showed our class the movie *Shattered Glass*, which she'd also asked her students to watch via Netflix in 2020, demonstrating the story's timelessness and worth for truth-telling scribes. The movie is based on former journalist Stephen Glass, who in real life made up the details of a series of stories he wrote in *The New Republic* in the 1990s. Glass wrote in a flashy, entertaining way, but many of his articles proved to be fabricated, and his unraveling in the movie is an astounding thing to witness.

"The shortcuts aren't there," McDonald reminded me when we reflected on the viewing of *Shattered Glass*. "And half the time it's easier to have done it the right way than it would be to fake it. But he was faking it in order to get the attention and to be buddies with everybody."

Some of the best advice on the basics of journalism that I received during my master's program came from Martin and McDonald in the Reporting I class. Because this is a book on how to do journalism right, I would like to share some of their thoughts. It's a long list of bullets that I extracted from my notes in graduate school. I think aspiring journalists will find these tips to be useful.

- Journalists must make it their mission to tell people what's going on by proactively thinking of who, what, where, why, how, and so what? Expect the unexpected and be a watchdog.
- News is the rough first draft of history, current and often unusual. News is fresh and valuable, something not known to the public before, and stories that people want and need.
- Don't patronize or lecture readers. Keep the focus on citizens.
- Dimensions of journalism include timeliness, news, public safety, crime, empowerment, identity, government, education, spirituality, human interest, drama, conflict, recognition, and editorializing.
- Journalists have a sense of obligation and responsibility. They put things in context and in perspective. They convey what happens, what it means, and why it's important. Journalists are more than just stenographers … say more than just what happened.
- News is about people, so find the human element, even in straight news stories about politics, education, and government. How do these things affect society? Focus on the substance of the story.
- Don't write about people in a cosmic sense; write about people using specifics. Sort out and make sense of what can be complicated stories about real people.
- Good journalists can get the news out there quickly and accurately, 24/7, though it's okay to get fresh news out after the competition does to make sure it's accurate.

- Get close to the story by leaving your office and computer. Think about where you might find people to get a great story.
- Curiosity is important for journalists. They must nurture it and develop it, asking questions and delving into issues and areas within those issues that others might not think of.
- Local news offers a sense of a community's identity.
- Pay attention to what people do outside of your community, and then see if the same situations could possibly affect where you live. Take national news and localize it.
- Journalists don't know the answers. Don't presume, and don't be opinionated.
- Objectivity for journalists means the science of reporting—gathering, testing, and presenting the info they attain. Talk thoroughly to enough people and ask hard questions. Trust but verify.
- Never forget how you or a family member would feel if a particularly sensitive news story was written about one of you. Would you object to the content or pictures? Write in a way that people don't get hurt. Every part of journalism has a moral and ethical part to it.
- Think of proximity when reporting. Journalists should focus on news that is close to them, but not overly so. In an opposite manner, readers want to see how national news affects their towns.
- The deeper the story's meaning, the deeper it will affect people.
- Stand up for the repressed.
- Adapt to unforeseen circumstances and stay calm.
- Get the dog's name in a story. The little things and the details count.
- Be skeptical, not cynical.
- The perils of reporters being around and talking to the same people are that they don't get different perspectives and may form biases. Journalists should set biases aside and learn from people's varied perspectives so they don't write too provincially.
- The quotes in a story can go beyond just the subject you're writing about.
- The quotes in a story aren't the nuts and bolts of the piece, but they do convey what people think and offer a sense of feeling.
- Sources in articles must be credible, accessible, and relevant to the subject at hand.
- Sources in a story must drive the article forward. Don't just use the first source you come in contact with if it doesn't help the story. Ask yourself why you're using a particular source; use a variety of sources if possible (e.g., experts and regular people).
- Don't use quotes from other publications. Do use other publications, however, for possible sources you can utilize.
- "Off the record" means different things to different publications. Editors typically want to know whom the source is.
- When considering sources for a story, think of the obvious ones first. The footnotes in Wikipedia entries are a good place to check for sources, as are the web pages of companies, institutions, and government entities.
- Excel is an outstanding repository for acquired sources.

- Using the present tense for a story can work, but there must be a reason for doing it that way. Stories are generally in past tense.
- Use fewer words and use the best possible words that are down to earth. Avoid jargon and write stories in a readable way. Be concise with language; write tight.
- Mix up paragraph lengths, the language, and the writing style. Write in a way that flows like a good musical beat. *How* you present your story can keep people reading.
- Write lots more than you need for your story and pick out the best things. Get so much great material that you have to leave some good stuff out.
- Allow citizens to respond to stories and be sure to report on the progress, or lack of progress, on a covered topic. Focus on solutions to problems and keep people's attention on the problems. Try to answer the question, "What's next?"
- See your subject in action and pound the pavement. Overhear and discover new things. Stories with the most legwork are the best ones.
- Include unique parts of the story if there are any (e.g., a truck hits a firetruck that was responding to a call that turned out to be a false alarm).
- Talk to people in person or at least on the phone.
- Develop relationships with key people and utilize social media to monitor what people are doing and thinking.
- The Internet is an outstanding resource, but be sure to talk to people in person.
- Use attribution when an opinion is offered or when something is subjective. Attribution also helps when you need to back up outlandish or controversial statements or when there is no eyewitness knowledge.
- Attribution can also be used to confirm something such as an arrest (e.g., according to the Champaign Police Department).
- Attribution in a story gives it validity and can help protect against libel claims.
- Make your questions to interviewees conversational but not wordy. Keep the questions short and ask follow-up questions when needed. Silence is an acceptable mechanism when subjects are afraid to answer tough questions.
- Don't be intimidating when interviewing children. Pull up a chair and try to make them feel comfortable. Make *everyone* feel comfortable when you interview them. That's how you get the best quotes.
- Listen to people when they talk—it's an act of humility.
- Don't rely on your memory. Use a tape recorder or digital recorder when interviewing people, and make sure the batteries are working. Bring extra batteries with you.
- Sometimes people who go through difficult periods in their lives want to talk about those difficulties. Don't be afraid to ask them about these issues, but be polite. Well-known people are willing to talk, too.
- Be quiet when doing interviews, but remain engaged. You're not there to be someone's friend, but a good relationship doesn't hurt.
- Always be polite to people's secretaries or handlers.
- Ask questions when covering government-related stories. Don't take answers at face value. Question authority.
- Many stories have a money angle; never forget that.
- Get permission to use photos and information on social media.

- Consider including the age of a person for ID purposes, especially if the person has a common name.
- Learn about leads, the inverted pyramid style of writing, and what makes good quotes.
- Learn from your mistakes, talk to firsthand sources, double check everything, check your math, and know how to do the math.
- Document what you report and attribute information correctly. The more sources you have the better.
- The five freedoms within the First Amendment are freedom of the press, freedom of religion, the right to assemble, the right to petition government, and the right to free speech.
- Good journalists are fair, impartial, and connected to the world so that they can see all sides of an issue. Don't theorize until after you have all the data you need.
- Truth and accuracy are the best defenses against libel, but journalists must be able to prove the information in their pieces is accurate by recording conversations, taking good notes, corroborating facts, double checking facts, and talking to everyone who is involved with the story.
- Be especially careful when reporting police and court stories. Routine stories are the ones that most often result in libel charges. There are no little stories.
- Make corrections promptly if there are mistakes. Don't dismiss people who say something is incorrect.
- Is your story accurate? Is it fair? Is it derogatory? Pay attention, get it right, and have fun!

Chapter 2: Working the Beat

Once upon a time, newspapers hired writers for specialized topics they became experts in. Comparable to how community policing by cops on a particular "beat" builds familiarity and trust among citizens, beat reporters for newspapers cover specific areas of news and build invaluable relationships with trusted sources to write explanatory, dependable stories. Newspaper readers benefit from the knowledge of beat reporters, who help keep community members abreast of important topics.

But with newspapers in decline for so long, beat reporting has suffered. When layoffs in journalism occur, beat reporters are often the first to be let go, according to a 2018 question-and-answer piece by The Conversation titled "Why the Demise of Specialist Reporters is a Loss for Any Democracy." In the Q&A session conducted by Natasha Joseph, scholar Glenda Daniels said the increasing absence of beat journalists worldwide means that important issues, often in rural areas, aren't getting the coverage they deserve.

The move toward digitized news and the rise of social media have led to cutbacks on beat reporting, according to Daniels, who said that coverage in Australia of indigenous groups has been more prominent via Twitter and academics than by mainstream-media beat reporters.

In his 2017 book, *The Death of Expertise: The Campaign Against Established Knowledge and Why it Matters*, Tom Nichols argues that the ultra-quick access to information that many people have these days has hampered debate and cheapened the knowledge of intellectuals and experts. With so much information seemingly supporting all viewpoints, everyone knows everything and all views must be taken seriously—or else, Nichols says. The Amazon promo copy for the book reads:

Tom Nichols' The Death of Expertise *shows how this rejection of experts has occurred: the openness of the internet, the emergence of a customer satisfaction model in higher education, and the transformation of the news industry into a 24-hour entertainment machine, among other reasons. Paradoxically, the increasingly democratic dissemination of information, rather than producing an educated public, has instead created an army of ill-informed and angry citizens who denounce intellectual achievement. When ordinary citizens believe that no one knows more than anyone else, democratic institutions themselves are in danger of falling either to populism or to technocracy or, in the worst case, a combination of both.*

I believe some aspects of Nichols' theory correlate to what has harmed journalism: the free-ranging online world where readers can view only the articles they want, by the publications they prefer; bloggers, pundits, and academics who see only their facts and leave little room for a civilized exchange of ideas; and 24-hour news cycles with aggressive pundits who speculate daily.

Given these changes in journalism, community beat reporters covering areas such as education, crime, and government for cash-strapped newspapers in some ways seems like quaint journalistic practices of yesteryear. An April 2020 article by the Pew Research Center, "U.S. newspapers have shed half of their newsroom employees since 2008," relates the sobering facts for newspaper journalists. Among them: between 2008 and 2019, those employed in U.S. newsrooms declined by 23%; during the same period, the number of newspaper journalists within newsrooms fell by 51%, from 71,000 employees to 35,000; and the number of newspapermen and women in newsrooms fell from six in ten individuals in 2008 to four in ten by 2019.

On the positive side, according to the piece, employment since 2008 in news mediums such as TV, cable, radio, and digital-native formats has remained steady, with impressive job growth in the digital-native sector, which has more than doubled during the same period. Nonetheless, from January 2017 to April 2018, one-fourth of digital-native news sites reported laying off their journalists. That's not as troubling as one-third of large U.S. newspapers doing the same thing, but it was unexpected.

To be sure, there are still plenty of beat writers and investigative journalists uncovering stories and producing good work. Brant Houston, the Knight Chair Professor in Investigative and Enterprising Reporting in the College of Media at Illinois, noted the dramatic increase of nonprofit newsrooms during the last decade as a bright spot in journalism, though he knows journalists in these organizations are stretched thin, sometimes beyond even their creative duties.

"Everyone's thinking about all these parts," Houston said. "Earned revenue, do we take advertising? Sponsorship? By the way, we've got to do really good stories so we have great content, which is why we originally do it—so we have something that people really should support."

Houston said *The News-Gazette*, as a midsize paper in Champaign-Urbana, has had to decide what is truly important to print since it has fewer journalists. As a result, he said, important city council stories may go by the wayside.

"A lot of the small to medium newspapers, there may be alleged beats, but they've kind of disappeared," said Houston, who estimated the paper has gone from approximately twenty reporters to just five in the past few years.

In a 2018 *Columbia Journalism Review* piece titled "As newsrooms do more with less, can reporters keep up?" writer Jared Brey describes the popular practice of newsrooms tracking the metrics of journalists' published stories to gauge which articles are the most popular. According to the article, writers are required to churn out pieces at a high rate while paying close attention to their page views. In-depth stories on important topics are often neglected as journalists feel the pressure to churn out as many click-bait stories as possible, with the number of clicks top of mind.

Is this the way to better reporting?

Not according to a January 2018 piece by Martha Waggoner, "Click Goals: For journalists, the pressure is always there. But are they improving reporting?" She writes in the article that newspapers "complain of goals that are too high and require too many stories, given the severely reduced size of newsrooms staffs. And they say the goals hinder quality journalism because reporters focus on stories that will get a lot of hits, such as one with a tangential connection to a celebrity or one that includes photos of pets. In the meantime, reporters say they are abandoning or being told to abandon beats that don't come with a deep readership, such as prisons or certain neighborhoods."

Houston said content should be the top priority whether a newspaper is for-profit or nonprofit, the latter of which entails a donation model that has been successful for publications in recent years.

"You're not going to get donations for garbage," said Houston, who taught the Reporting II class I took in 2013. "And so, I think it's been, to some degree, a self-correcting system. If people are just sitting there trying to see how many people would read their story and so forth, it corrupts the content. It's like you can sell a lot of really terrible sneakers that fall apart in a month. Eventually, it's going to catch up with you."

No class in my journalism master's program was more diversified than Brant Houston's Reporting II class (JOUR 415). Looking back at the material now, it's amazing how much we covered, read, and wrote.

It started with picking the type of beat you wanted to pursue for the semester—mine was education, and I covered the topic of truancy in schools. I wrote a story on an agency called Access Initiative of Champaign County, which, as of this writing, continues to assist troubled youth in the area. I wrote another article titled "Curbing school truancy takes effort on various fronts." My lead highlighted a child named J'von Coleman, who overslept and biked 30 miles to get to school. The first sentence in the article reads, "Anyone despondent about chronic absenteeism issues in today's public schools might find the recent story of J'von Coleman to be heartwarming."

I wrote a profile piece that semester titled "Teacher still dedicated despite struggles with cutbacks," which Houston thought was good enough to publish on *C-U Citizen Access*, an online community news project that he oversees. The teacher featured in the piece was Darla Frye, who now goes by Darla Deakin. We met on a brisk October evening at a coffee shop in town that's now closed, and she told me about the good and bad aspects of her occupation. We covered chronically absent children who attended her school, which at the time didn't have a major problem with that issue. But Deakin lamented how a lack of school funding was causing programs and positions, including social workers, to disappear.

"They're spread so thin it's not even funny," Deakin said in the article. "That is the one thing that I think I would say I was passionate about. When we have all these kids with all these problems and never, never are they getting someone to sit down one on one."

The day after the piece was published, the principal at Deakin's Urbana school gave her an earful about offering some of her not-so-upbeat opinions. I felt bad for putting her in that spot, but the experienced teacher, who was also my friend, told me not to worry about it— she had a right to say what she wanted to say.

Houston had a successful career as an investigative journalist, and that's the type of journalism we covered in his class. He struck me as a busy, accomplished guy and often had a preoccupied air, as if he needed to be somewhere else ten minutes ago, even as he was delivering a class lecture. But Houston's hard-driving work ethic was inspiring, and he was extremely knowledgeable.

He used to have us write "advance memos" in preparation for the topics and papers we were writing for our beats, to make sure we were on the right track. One time that semester he recommended I check in with the Center for Education in Small Urban Communities at the College of Education, thinking it would be a good way for me to get certain statistics. Funnily enough, the following semester I would go on to work at that college.

"You are now a beat reporter," read the first sentence of a handout Houston gave us. "You need to write me a memo off your beat that includes at least five sources that you believe you should contact on a regular basis to get story ideas and to stay atop what is occurring on your beat. In your memo, you need to explain your rationale for each source choice and include the individuals' names, phone numbers and email addresses."

At the bottom of the sheet, under a "Looking ahead:" subhead, Houston wrote, "Next week, you will have to provide five story ideas from your beat, including why these are viable stories, who your sources would be (names for at least three people and general descriptions of other possible sources) and what photos and/or video might be appropriate for telling this story."

My advance memos to Houston were crisp, no-nonsense write-ups in which I occasionally inserted personal thoughts. One memo reads:

My guess is that there are other schools in Urbana that are struggling with losing this truancy grant money. I would like to talk to people at a few Urbana schools, as well as with David Adcock, who is the director of Urbana Adult Education. In [Meg] Dickinson's N-G article, Adcock said "the schools' truancy outreach workers were often the parents' first point of contact in the schools." These workers kept documents and records that detailed how the schools were attempting to get kids to school, and they kept track of what the regional office and the state's attorney office were doing to fight the problem. Dickinson's article touches on this but doesn't go in depth, since her story was an overview of school truancy in C-U and Vermilion County.

Along with writing an advance memo for Deakin's story, I also churned out advanced memos for an "Agency that's not working" piece, and for my issues and overview stories on chronic truancy. These exercises made everything feel more official, as if we were real-life journalists working for an editor who wanted genuine scoops. Following the stories we wrote, Houston would have us write self-critiques on our pieces, which I think was immensely helpful. Rereading these critiques now, I see how they helped connect the stories we wrote while revealing to Houston what we were learning throughout the semester. In essence, we *were* reporting on our progress to an editor, helping him understand our reporting mindsets and reflecting on how we might proceed with future pieces. Here's the final paragraph I wrote in my self-critique on the overview article on truancy:

This article continually improved as I revised it, thanks to the advice of Ron Meador, Walt Harrington and others in Chapter 6 of "The Investigative Reporter's Handbook." What started out as a dry, statistically focused story evolved into one with a lead that at least contains a humanistic feel, while quotes from officials later in the piece offer in-the-trenches insights. My goal for future JOUR 415 stories is to aim higher all the way around: the best possible sources, stimulating stories by real people, pertinent facts that open some eyes and documents that may reveal flaws in the system.

Houston wrote one of our class textbooks, the aforementioned *The Investigative Reporter's Handbook: A Guide to Documents, Databases and Techniques.* The book is a must-have for any aspiring, and currently working, investigative reporter. Here's what I wrote about the first several assigned chapters:

This book begins by describing what investigative journalism is, how the definition of the craft has evolved and, probably most importantly, what it entails. Good journalists in this line of work are curious and full of questions, healthily skeptical and persistent in acting on behalf of the public good. With hard work investigative journalists can make big discoveries.

Chapter 1 lists the 11 common-sense steps it takes to potentially pursue a story, but to me, the most helpful paragraphs were on pages 6 and 7. I've never written in a "document state of mind" before, so I was curious about the best way to meld the official documentation with the human part of the story (the interviews). It's clearly explained in "The Investigative Reporter's Handbook" that the documents a journalist finds can dictate what the interview questions will be, and can help keep the interviewees honest. I now view investigative journalism as writing a story based on official documents, with the appropriate interviewees coloring the article later with their thoughts that can either back up or contradict the information.

In Chapter 2, readers learn about the wealth of secondary sources available to help write articles, which may be more familiar than the sources from computer-assisted research covered in later chapters. Secondary sources include newspapers, magazines, newsletters, academic papers and books. It was interesting to read about author Jessica Mitford's insights into the differences between a publication that is for public and private consumption. A journalist would want to get his hands on an organization's internal publication.

Online search techniques are also covered, and it's evident that there are underlying layers to the web, beyond Google, where reporters can gather relevant info. It was helpful to learn about the website at aip.completeplanet.com, where specialized search engines and searchable databases are available.

Chapter 4, "Computer-Assisted Reporting," offers writers numerous ways to find web-based resources on well-known subjects. Many are aware of the evolving, high-tech media platforms available today, but less people may know about the plethora of ways journalists can attain information – even established journalists may not know all the resources they have at their fingertips nowadays.

The Investigative Reporters and Editors website offers aspiring and established journalists a multitude of ways to better their craft and enhance their knowledge on available resources. The site is filled with many investigative articles that give writers a sense of what stories in society may go uncovered and what to look for when covering them. Additionally, IRE has a plethora of "tipsheets" that members can access for advice. One currently posted tip is labeled "10 tips for doing great work in challenging times."

A section of the site labeled NICAR & Data Library specializes in training journalists on how to attain electronic information and has available databases for purchase for IRE members.

Seven years after taking my class with Houston, he said investigative journalism is in a good place thanks to the rise of nonprofit newsrooms.

"The nonprofit newsroom movement really got going because investigative reporters at metropolitan dailies, and other places but particularly there, were not able to do investigative work at the quality level they wanted to, or they were laid off," Houston said. "So, what happened is that the people moved to nonprofit newsrooms, especially initially. [They] were looking to increase the amount of watchdog enterprises, meaningful investigative work."

Houston's class was full of hands-on activities that revealed what dedicated journalists need to do to get detailed stories. While in his class, I wrote an FOIA (Freedom of Information Act) letter to the Champaign Unit 4 School District, interviewed numerous professionals in the education field, and wrote several articles on a topic—chronic truancy—that I began to care more and more about.

Houston had an artier side to him, I think, which may have explained his interest in literary journalism and its surprising similarities to investigative journalism. The books he assigned us to read covered a wide range of topics—some you might expect to see in a Reporting II class, some not. We read parts of the massive tome *The Power Broker* by Robert A. Caro and delved into *The Working Poor* by David K. Shipler, which I described in an essay as "densely written." We also read *The Art of Access* by David Cuillier and Charles N. Davis, as well as James C. Foust's *Online Journalism*, which offered fantastic information for aspiring journalists who were increasingly working in a more tech-heavy environment.

But by far my favorite book that Houston assigned was *Behind the Beautiful Forevers* by Katherine Boo, a riveting nonfiction read that—sorry for the cliché—reads like a novel. Here's how I described the book in a class essay:

Beautiful Forevers is one of those books that could be life-changing for some. The stories within it have the power to conjure melancholy, helplessness and thankfulness for what you have. It's possibly inspired others to help make a difference in the world. Amazingly, amid all the smoke, grime, death, backward ways, sickness, corruption and poverty within this "undercity" in huge Mumbai, Boo writes with a sheen and poeticism that somehow lets beauty in. The sheer will of some of these Indians is even more impressive.

To capture these events, Boo immersed herself in Annawadi, a slum where squatters live, just outside the Mumbai airport. An undercurrent of concern among Annawadians – among lots of day-to-day struggles – is the looming fear that their shacks will be razed in the future by airport officials who own the land. As planes land and take off from the Mumbai airport that is surrounded by luxurious hotels, Annawadians hardly get by. Merely getting water for the household can take hours of standing in line. A highly polluted lake, fighting among neighbors and dirty communal toilets are also aspects of life in Annawadi.

Boo's observed circumstances are brutal, but what makes this book riveting is its characters: Abdul, the silent garbage collector who strives to remain above the sordid fray of society; Manju, a pretty college girl whose future and virtuousness seem to erode each time readers catch up with her; Manju's mother, who lends a supposed helpful public hand, for personal gain only; and the cursed Hussain family, whose legal troubles demonstrate the pervasive issues that poor people must deal with from crooked cops and an archaic judicial system, inside jail cells that are unfit for the wrongly and rightly accused.

Though it's not fair to paint diverse and evolving India in one broad stroke, this sliver of Annawadian life in the big city had common issues that Boo witnessed in other poor regions of the country. Those issues include a lack of opportunities and rights for those in poverty; Hindu-Muslim fighting and shady political dealings; and a level of disrespect and minimal options for women that is unbelievable to witness in today's world. Spotty electricity, sparse running water, and inadequate housing and hospitals are other issues. India's horrific caste system is being replaced by a "global market" mentality that inspires personal gain but also highlights how competitive and uncaring the world is.

The fact that Boo had the fortitude to pull off this brand of immersion journalism was brilliant, courageous and good for the world. Not since reading the novel A Fine Balance *by Rohinton Mistry – also about India – have I been this moved by people's circumstances in a book.*

One afternoon in the lab portion of Reporting II, Houston shared his in-depth knowledge about Excel spreadsheets, which can be used as a platform for data analysis and data visualization. Houston said journalists should embrace information and hone their math skills if they are interested in making good money as data reporters. Skillfully finding and downloading data and exporting it to a spreadsheet or database manager can lead to creating maps more effectively and doing in-depth analyses on social networks, as just a few examples.

Janelle O'Dea is a data reporter and journalist with the *St. Louis Post-Dispatch* now, but when she was in Houston's class with me, both of us were a little overwhelmed by the data aspect of journalism. But Janelle, who wanted to be a journalist after graduation, knew she had to learn what Houston was teaching. She graduated from Illinois in 2014 and continues to hone her data-seeking skills.

"Even still today I feel like I'm behind," O'Dea told me. "You've got to keep up with it, with technology and *The New York* Times and *The Washington Post*, with the stuff they're doing way beyond what we're doing here at the *Post-Dispatch*. So that's a constant struggle of feeling like you're behind and you're always trying to catch up."

Before taking Houston's course, I had met Janelle three years prior at *The News-Gazette*, where we were part-time telemarketers with a passion for writing. Janelle told me when we spoke via Zoom that her over-the-phone newspaper-selling skills left a lot to be desired.

But she is an outstanding journalist who got her start early on as the newspaper editor at Mahomet-Seymour High School. Later she wrote for *The Prospectus* at Parkland College. At the U of I, Janelle worked with Houston to do an investigative piece about dilapidated Greek houses on campus and the dangers they posed to their inhabitants.

Janelle told me the thrill of seeing her byline was at first the "selfish thing" that appealed to her about being a journalist, but she quickly discovered that the public-service side of journalism was an even bigger reward. As an example, she mentioned a *Post-Dispatch* story she had recently written, "'Worst thing we've ever seen': Thousands of evictions loom in St. Louis," a pertinent topic to many in St. Louis.

"I realized it could be a dual-purpose life," Janelle said about following her passion for writing. "Getting my work and my writing published, and also helping keep governments accountable and making sure people aren't getting the short end of the stick."

Her stories "based on analysis" are her favorite ones, she said. Such articles sprout from an initial curiosity on a particular issue within St. Louis or in Missouri. Data is compiled to decipher possible trends, and sometimes the information is so compelling that it ends up being an easy-to-write nut graph the piece is based on.

"Some stories just almost write themselves," Janelle said. "The dataset comes to me and there are so many good points in there that lead us to so many different anecdotes."

The article contributions of a data reporter like Janelle vary. Sometimes she'll write the entire piece or most of it, with fellow reporters contributing a few paragraphs. Other times she'll contribute a lone sentence to a story, or perhaps provide a map or chart, visual elements that lend their own specialized angles to an article. Janelle calls interactive maps and other forms of multimedia that contribute to a story the "new frontier of journalism."

According to Janelle, data reporters interact with every beat writer in the newsroom. An education beat writer, for instance, may seek her out to discover what local school had the highest student enrollment during the last year, along with the percentage of students the school had of the total enrollment number in the school district. Oftentimes, she said, the information she churns out is so enticing that her editor will assign the story to Janelle rather than to a beat writer. Sometimes both she and the beat reporter will collaborate, with Janelle contributing the data-driven content and the beat expert contributing his knowledge on the topic. All contributing writers are recognized at the end of these types of pieces.

Janelle has dug up data for the *Post-Dispatch* that have appeared in various series of stories the newspaper has published, some of which have been investigative pieces. Of course, the *Post-Dispatch* also prints feature stories that are more personal, articles in which cold-sounding data also have a place. Janelle mentioned the paper's six-part series on the bleakness and horrors of dementia as an example, saying even in articles that evoke deep emotions, pointed data still have a place.

"Marrying those two things can be difficult, but there's almost always a spot in a story where you are going to have broader context, and where you can get at where our state fits into the national, where the national fits into the world, or here's where our county fits into the state," she said.

Like numerous newspapers nationwide, the *Post-Dispatch* has gone through tough times. The publication's spacious longtime downtown headquarters was leased out in 2019 to Square Inc., a Silicon Valley company co-founded by Jack Dorsey and Jim McKelvey. A quote on the wall by Joseph Pulitzer was kept on the former *Post-Dispatch* building as a tribute to the newspaper and to its past and current employees, the latter of whom were asked to move to what Janelle said is an "ugly 1980s nondescript office building" not far from where she formerly worked. Those walking into the building can still see Pulitzer's inspiring words.

"You know what would have been a better tribute?" Janelle said. "Just let us stay there."

It took more than a year to get a *Post-Dispatch* sign installed on the 1980s-looking building, according to Janelle, but she said the move did have some benefits: staff members received a new coffee machine and chairs.

Houston once recommended in class to read anything you can get your hands on. When I interviewed him seven years later, he told me he'd recently heard three esteemed journalists give the same advice at different conferences: read, they advised. Reading can get reporters in a "documents state of mind," according to Houston, and "helps you break through this veneer of the familiar."

"I think reading and the habit of reading makes you a better writer, a better teller of stories," Houston said. "Reading also opens your eyes to all sorts of information that's coming across that is not intended as a press release, that is not intended as a message targeting you. It's a way to get out of your bubble. And it's a basic thing of reporting."

Another time Houston said in class that Champaign County was in the "dark ages" when it came to the information it made available to reporters and citizens. I was sitting right by him when he volunteered that opinion and didn't raise my hand to ask him why he thought that. When I asked him about it seven years later via Zoom, Houston told me restaurant inspections were not made public when he moved to Champaign-Urbana, and that Champaign is one of the few counties in central Illinois where people cannot do a public online search of a property by the name of the property owner.

Houston added that access to information in the county has improved somewhat in recent years, and he believes his journalism students writing for CU-CitizenAccess.org have played a role in helping with that.

Houston said that when he first began teaching "computer-assisted reporting," it was difficult to convince his students to stop interviewing people for a second and look at a computer screen to try to accumulate valuable data. Now he has the opposite problem.

"It's hard to get people off the screen and on the street to talk to people," he said. "More and more, I say the three pillars of journalism are documents-data, interviews, and observation. I want everybody to see, to experience all three of those things."

These are facets of journalism I remember well from Reporting II. Here is what I wrote in the summation essay to conclude the semester:

The most helpful things I learned in JOUR 415 is how official documents and records can supplement and enhance the validity of a story, help journalists find or write a story and can be used as a means to ask human sources the right questions. The sheer amount of online help to attain documents is nearly overwhelming, but for practicing reporters who know where to look, they are invaluable. The phrase "documents state of mind" perfectly sums up a big part of this course.

We covered the numerous kinds of human sources, which include experts, witnesses, former and current workers, people affected by the issue, spokespeople and advocates. Similarly, primary documents (originals), meeting notes, public notices in newspapers, police and court records and footnotes in publications can be helpful to journalists in different ways. One little data point can possibly lead to a big story.

Through an assigned reading and the lectures, this course showed how to request Freedom of Information documents, and during the semester I asked for – and received – two of them. (One contained statistics that were especially helpful for my overview story.) It was interesting to learn about the various dynamics between journalists who request FOIs and the government officials who are sometimes cautious about releasing them. These relationships can range from friendly to hostile, and journalists have to be prepared to negotiate with different types of people who have information they need.

Being a savvy web user, which isn't hard to be, is a key way to know how to find needed data on websites. Organizations post a great deal of information about themselves these days, so it pays to look for things like minutes from meetings, financial information, newsletters and annual reports before contacting anybody for assistance with locating them. Through this course, I truly got a sense of how the web can be a great tool to get information on people and organizations. Reporters should build up a library of websites to utilize.

Along those lines, I now pay more attention to things like maps that accompany online news articles, as well as videos that go with stories. There is no doubt that journalism has evolved into an entity in which several media platforms regularly convey information in different ways, and on-the-go devices such as cell phones have significantly changed how news is released to the world.

One of the first lectures conveyed how reporting is a state of mind that never stops. Journalists should be on constant alert for interesting story ideas, trying to figure out how things work and why. Though it's hard to do, reporters can't go to work every day with the same mindset. If they do, they may miss a good story right in front of their faces. Making the "invisible" people visible should be a goal of good journalists. Additionally, as a reporter, it's okay to form a hypothesis going into a story, but be sure to keep an open mind and practice diligent reporting so that preconceived notions don't influence the truth.

We were told to think of our stories in this class as a "package," and I think that is a good way to view them. For my own beat of chronic truancy and the school system in general, I learned things from story to story that determined the direction of my articles along the way. I can see how reporters on a specific beat would want to cultivate human sources that could help them with relevant info as their beat evolved. Knocking on doors and visiting with individuals on the front lines of an organization are solid ways to start.

Interviewing tips in the class were wide-ranging and helpful, from putting your phone number in the email signature line to doing thorough research on an interviewee before the interview. To get the interview, journalists should try to convey to people that something is in it for them; they can tell their side of the story, which is good if it's a narrow issue that may not get covered otherwise. Reporters can "seduce" the interviewee by rehashing her accomplishments, which may flatter her and reveal that you've done your homework. It's important to try to make the whole interview process as convenient as possible for the person you're talking to. Meet with them when they can do it (provided there isn't an urgent deadline) and try to go where they want to go to talk. If the interview takes place over the phone, tell them it won't take long, and you can talk when it's convenient for them.

Other interviewing tips include being quiet at certain moments; steering the interview in the direction you want it to go if that's required; being flexible with your questions as the interview progresses; acting as "dumb" as possible so that you don't appear like you already know what's going to be said; and improvising along the way if needed. The best interviews are the ones that are more like conversations.

Following the shooting at LAX Airport in Los Angeles, we covered how reporters can prepare themselves to cover such tragedies. Creating a working contact list beforehand so that you are not caught off guard is helpful. When big news breaks it's essential to think like a reporter. Also, following the initial big story, it's important to think of relevant follow-up articles that could be written. In the Midwest, events like tornadoes qualify as an on-the-spot reporting story that may need covering, so reporters should be prepared. Other potential drawn up "reporters' plans" could be ones for truck spills, train and plane crashes and acts of terrorism.

Brant Houston did a great job of conveying to the class how journalists should be curious and want to read, and he demonstrated that by bringing in specific books to class one day. Reading material that may conflict with our own viewpoints, or reading about subjects that we may think we have no interest in or don't know anything about, are great ways to get story ideas or to simply learn for the sake of learning. Throughout the semester, Houston talked a lot about municipal subjects that may not interest some journalists because on the surface they seem boring. But great stories that benefit the public can be anywhere. It was good he brought up these topics to get us thinking about community-oriented happenings. I think his hard-nosed, dedicated, no-frills approach was something all of us needed to see, because journalists get good stories by being tenacious, digging deep, reading about current events and diving right in.

When this class concluded in December of 2013, it made me wonder what happened to everything I was doing—it seemed as if all the work just vanished. How could it all have ended so suddenly? The Reporting II course had an on-the-job feel, sort of like a part-time gig I wanted to continue. I think the activities I was doing in the class made me feel as if I was part of something larger than myself, and I didn't want that feeling to end.

I guess I had this unexpected hollowness inside when Houston's class ended.

Luckily, two more upcoming hands-on journalism courses were right around the corner to fill the void.

Chapter 3: Personal Conversations, Crimes, and a Helluva Story

In August of 2014—two years after purchasing my first graduate school textbook at the Illini Union Bookstore—I walked into a classroom on the third floor of Gregory Hall, Room 336. Every student who is lucky enough to attend college should also be fortunate enough to have a class in a space like Room 336—it emanates that sense of privilege one feels within the learning spaces of academia.

The first thing most people would likely notice when entering the room is the long wooden table, which sits atop a floral-patterned rug with a maroon-colored outline. Above the table is a white, modern-looking projector that hangs from the ceiling and is aimed at a screen that rolls down over the chalkboard at the front of the room. Majestic wood paneling adorns the white walls, which have a few hanging pictures with illustrations of campus buildings, one of them Greg Hall. Heavy drapes stand guard on the sides of tall windows, a few of which offer a nice view of South Wright Street. Four saucer-shaped lamps hang above the table, offering a warm glow for the many students and instructors who have carried on countless conversations in the room spanning decades.

The only thing Room 336 was missing was a fireplace to curl up next to and read. Observing the atmosphere on that summer day in 2014, I felt as if I were immediately becoming more scholarly through the osmosis of my surroundings. But I was also a bit intimidated.

A good number of students sat around the elongated table, and at first, I wondered if I would even be able to find a place to sit. I had to edge my way into a seat near the head of the table, where Professor Leon Dash held court, waiting patiently for everyone to settle in. After the bell in the outside hall rang, he proceeded to talk about immersion journalism.

During my graduate studies, I received numerous handouts in every class that contained invaluable advice on journalism. One of them, which I think was given to me in the Reporting I course, has a heading that reads "Interview tips." Following that are three categories titled "Setting up the interview," "Preparing yourself before the interview," and "During the interview," each with a slew of bullets underneath them. In all, there are twenty-seven bullets that span three pages.

These sheets provide outstanding advice for journalists—well, for beginning journalists, that is. But for reporters who want to truly explore the depths of the topics or people they're covering, the person to talk to—or take a class with—is Professor Leon Dash.

Like all the teachers I learned from during graduate school, Dash has an impressive background that gave him a distinguished air. One of his biggest accomplishments, as noted in his online College of Media bio, is the 1994 Pulitzer Prize for Explanatory Journalism he earned for a serial piece he wrote on poverty in America. He also earned a Robert F. Kennedy Journalism Award for this effort. Dash has an exciting, danger-filled international journalism background. From his online bio:

"Among his more thrilling early assignments were two prolonged periods of closely observing UNITA rebels in Angola, one for four months, and the second (during the brutal civil war in 1976) for seven months. Dash traveled a collective 2,500 miles on foot, mostly through a war zone. Besides giving Dash the qualifications for appointment as the West African Station Chief in 1979, these excursions put Dash in close proximity with his subject, which gave shape to his unique style of investigation."

Dash worked as a reporter at *The Washington Post* for thirty years. Along with winning a Pulitzer, he's written two noteworthy books, served in high positions at the College of Media, and in 2016 was inducted into the National Association of Black Journalists Founders Hall of Fame.

I remember Dash as this tall, patient, distinguished-looking professor at the end of the long table in Room 336, listening intently as each of his Immersion Journalism students talked about the subjects they were interviewing. I reconnected with Dash for this book to see if we could talk, and to see if he could email me the Immersion Journalism syllabus, which he did (I later found the copy I used for class). Except for the information about COVID-19, which dictates that students do their interviews via Skype or Zoom because of the pandemic, the content in the 14-page syllabus is exactly how I remember the class being. The first two paragraphs highlight what the course entails:

"This seminar will introduce you to the journalistic interview techniques of immersion journalism. The methodology examines contemporary social phenomena through the lives of individuals and families. The student will study an actual application of the methodology in the book, When Children Want Children, which is an examination of adolescent childbearing among high school students in a very poor neighborhood of Washington, D. C. You will learn the techniques by doing an actual project of your choosing. You will have to recruit a participant, interview the person extensively with a digital recorder, transcribe the interviews, and write a midterm and final story/narrative based on the interviews.

"The interview methodology you will use is seen as the best way to provide the ethnographer/writer/reporter with insight into social phenomena. The methodology can be used to examine the living conditions, family history and attitudes of any ethnic group at any class level -- wealthy, affluent, middle class, working class, poor or underclass."

Following the paragraph with the pandemic information, Dash wrote:

"The student with an insatiable curiosity about human behavior will be able to extract from willing participants surprising revelations about their needs, desires and motivations. Importantly, you will learn how the personalities, the circumstances, and the choices made by your participants' parents and forebears still have bearing on the life of your participant today. Often, an individual is unaware of the past's impact on their present-day life until your interviewing brings it to their attention. When this moment of self-awareness occurs and, if it is not too painful, your participant will likely become fully committed to YOUR project.

"How quickly a respondent will open up with the interviewer during the weeks-long interview process is determined by the nature of the student's inquiry, the personality of the participant and the developing interview skills of the student. Do not be intimidated. Skillful interviewers, much as is the case for good writers, are created through hard work. They are not adept questioners by birth.

"Whatever you may feel about the life choices made by your participant, it is important that you remain neutral -- try not to reveal negative judgment in your eyes or let a judgmental nuance slip into your speech -- during your interaction with the participant. If the participant sees or senses that you are judgmental, he or she will then tell you what the participant believes you find acceptable behavior, which may not be the behavior of the participant.

"In a short, semester-length course, it is prudent to stay away from difficult subjects when first trying out this methodology. For example, matters of human sexuality are delicate, and difficult to explore openly with persons of any culture and of any social background. Often, people will not feel comfortable talking on-the-record about their sexuality until they have been interacting with the interviewer for a period of four to six months. You do not have that much time so make a thoughtful choice about which social phenomenon you want to explore."

When I talked to Dash in 2020 via Zoom, I heard once again his from-the-belly laugh and enjoyed hearing his memorable stories from the past. In the late 1990s, he had his pick of several prestigious schools to teach at, but he chose Illinois for two reasons. First, the university offered him full professorship and tenure. Secondly, one of Dash's daughters has cerebral palsy, and he was highly impressed with the Division of Disability Resources & Educational Services (DRES) at the institution, one of the first programs in the U.S. to support students with disabilities.

Dash often said in class that you can learn a great deal about an individual by inquiring into these four areas of life: the person's history in school; the person's life within the family he or she grew up in; the role of religion, faith, or the absence of those things in a person's life; and the individual's life growing up outside of his or her family. Dash said that starting an interview with people in the realms of school, family, and faith opens them up and helps prevent canned responses. He said this is an especially helpful tactic with politicians and celebrities, who are used to answering the same questions repeatedly.

"Now, if you take them through—you sit them down, and they have the time and you have the time—from the first through the twelfth grade, you get a very different version," Dash said.

For a more in-depth, well-rounded talk with politicians and celebrities, Dash said journalists should spend fifteen minutes covering school history, fifteen minutes on family history, fifteen minutes on faith, and fifteen minutes on growing up outside the family. Doing so will result in "a very different interview," he said, because the individuals will reveal much more about themselves during the next portion of the talk.

"The second hour of the interview, what you will get from the person is very different than if you had started the second-hour interview with their life as a celebrity or with their life as a politician. Makes a big difference," Dash said.

School, religion, and life with and beyond the family. These were the aspects of a person's life I would have to probe in-depth on.

But first, I had to find somebody who was willing talk to me, and I mean really *talk*. And he or she had to be interesting. And I didn't have much time to find this individual.

In my next Immersion Journalism class, I saw right away there were noticeably fewer students sitting around the long table. The following class—same thing. As the classes rolled on, it became, unbelievingly, just me and five other students. We had this beautiful classroom and table all to ourselves. Dash said students often drop out in droves because they think Immersion Journalism will be a piece of cake. One look at the syllabus, however, and that fallacy disappears.

The same thing happened to Dash when he first began teaching the course in the spring semester of 1999, and it was surprising to him. On the first day of class, after handing out the syllabus, the students inquired if they could do the interviews by phone. Dash said no:

the interviews had to be done in person. He told his first group of Immersion Journalism students that in-person interviews were essential for truly getting to know the interviewees and seeing their mannerisms and reactions as words were exchanged. In-person interviews build trust, he said, and help journalists observe whether or not their subjects are being untruthful, though the absolute truth, in many instances, can be difficult to attain, according to Dash.

"So, the next time we met—I remember I started with eleven students—I had four students," Dash said of the 1999 class.

We talked *a lot* in Immersion Journalism, and Dash would listen intently, often interjecting with questions or suggestions on what we perhaps *should* have asked our subjects. My August 27 notes have advice such as "bring up your own experiences to get him to relate and talk"; "interviews should last around two hours at the start"; "be professional but don't hesitate to be social"; "human weakness: hard to keep a secret"; and "don't be vague when approaching people; get a commitment."

Dash's interviewing experience has shown him that contradictions in what interviewees say can begin to pop up between the third and fourth interviews covering faith and growing up outside of the family. This is because, he says, the subjects begin to feel more comfortable opening up and telling the truth as time goes on. He told us to not point out these contradictions, but rather to note them and ask follow-up questions later, with the objective of getting closer to the truest realities of the person. Interestingly, this element of an interview is one of Dash's favorite, most rewarding aspects of teaching Immersion Journalism.

"The revelation that the students experience in terms of when they realize that the person is contradicting what they originally told them, which I predict to most of the students that this is what will happen," Dash said.

But he warns students not to acknowledge and relate the contradictions to the interviewees. Instead, he said, "Be happy it appeared because now the person is beginning to tell you something that's closer to the truth."

A woman named Lolita Dumus, who assisted at an organization in town called Urbana Champaign Books to Prisoners, was the person who connected me to my interview subject in Immersion Journalism. As its name suggests, Books to Prisoners, which started in 2004, is a volunteer organization that provides books to incarcerated individuals. Back in August of 2014, it had provided nearly 100,000 books via nearly 29,000 packages to more than 15,000 inmates. As of this writing, those numbers have jumped to 167,489; 49,490; and 23,112, respectively.

Before committing any Books to Prisoners volunteers to my graduate school project, Dumus asked me to send her information on what the interview process during the semester would entail, and this is the message I sent via email:

Hi, Lolita -

Below is how the interview process would work throughout the semester and the topics covered. The interviews will be taped, and the interviewee has the right to request that any future articles may or may not be published, provided the articles are deemed worthy of publication by the professor.

General interview with subject about his life today, covering basic info such as work, interests, children, age, origin of family, and how long they've lived in the area. Collecting date of birth and contact info. This would also be a chance to explain to the interviewee the nature of the project and the commitment involved. This interview will probably be fairly short.

Second interview will cover school history year by year and earliest childhood memories.

Third interview will cover the subject's experience growing up inside his family. More childhood memories.
Fourth interview will cover the role of religion, faith, or absence of faith, as the case may be.
Fifth interview will cover topics of growing up independent outside of the family.

Three focused interviews that focus on what the theme of the final story will be. Whereas the previous interviews (2 through 4 above) may take up to two hours, these final three interviews won't be as long and as involved. We could even conduct them while having a meal somewhere. They may cover questions that weren't asked previously.

A definite time commitment would be required by the interviewee, as you can see, but I want this to be a fun process for both of us! Hopefully the interviews will seem more like conversations than formal get-togethers, just two people getting to know one another.

Let me know if you have any questions, and thanks again for your help.

Sal

Not long after, Dumus heard from a woman named Nancy Roberts of Jesus is the Way Prison Ministry in Rantoul. Individuals who work at this organization visit prisons and correctional institutions to spread the word of God to incarcerated individuals. Some of the prisoners they meet, upon release, are selected to be housed at Jesus is the Way, where they receive shelter, food, and clothing. But the ministry doesn't stop there. It also offers counseling, spiritual guidance, drug and alcohol rehabilitation for those who need it, as well as job-skill training and possible job placement. I visited this ministry several times during the semester and received nothing but positive vibes from it, both from the guys who lived there and the atmosphere in general.

Nancy Roberts emailed Dumus, who forwarded the message to me about an individual at Jesus is the Way named Louis, whom Roberts said was willing to participate in my Immersion Journalism project. Louis's upcoming schedule gave me a sense of how the ministry tries to keep its occupants busy throughout the days. Louis had a Monday through Friday job but would be at Hessel Park for a potluck on Saturday, September. 6. On the following day, he would be at the ministry in Rantoul for only three and a half hours, which made me think the rest of his day was occupied. Louis would also be available to chat with me for our initial interview at a New Horizon Church picnic, where, Roberts wrote, "He will be one of our guys by the 2 hogs pulling the pork off the hog." I decided to meet Louis at Hessel Park, probably just as intrigued to see the "2 hogs" as I was my future interviewee.

Roberts told me in her email that the men in Jesus is the Ways Ministry would be wearing purple shirts near the Hessel Park pavilion; so that's where I headed with my ten-year-old stepson, Logan. Following my brief first interview with Louis, Logan and I would head to the Illinois football game, just down the street at Memorial Stadium, where the Fighting Illini were playing the Western Kentucky Hilltoppers.

It was a hot sunny day. I parked across the street from Hessel, in the parking lot of a beloved Champaign ice cream place called Jarlings Custard Cup. Logan and I crossed Kirby Avenue and hustled to the pavilion. Hessel Park is a large, grassy area in the center of town with sidewalks all around it. It used to have an old, sharply angled red fire engine that kids could climb all over, but that playground liability is long gone. Many people who attend Illinois home football games park around the circumference of the sprawling Hessel Park because it's not too far of a walk to the stadium and parking is free. The town always feels abuzz on football Saturdays, even though the Illini football team has struggled for years, and that energy was present at Hessel Park the day I met Louis.

As Roberts had promised, the guys from the ministry were wearing purple T-shirts, making them easy to spot. I didn't know what he looked like, but it didn't take me long to locate Louis—I likely just asked someone where he was. He was sitting on the south side of the pavilion, not far from the tennis courts. Louis struck me right away as easygoing and accommodating. We decided it would be quieter to talk away from the group and headed toward the tennis courts to chat. With Logan in tow, gamely willing to sit through an interview with a man I'd just met, we sat down on the grass, where I pressed the record button on a blue tape recorder I was using at the time.

Louis Postlewaite was a fifty-seven-year-old black man. He had a round, bald head and deep lines on his forehead and on the sides of his mouth. A light mustache grazed his upper lip, and a thin line of short white hair rounded out the bottom half of his face. In the only photo I ever took of him during our time together, captured at a fast-food restaurant (I think it was McDonald's), Louis's eyes have a pained look. He didn't smile or laugh often, but on the rare occasions that he did, I noticed his front teeth were twisted, a contrast to his perfectly shaped dome.

Prior to doing our first interviews, Professor Dash asked the class for a "progress report" on relevant topics surrounding our interviewees. I wrote a piece titled "The Impact of Literacy on Lost Lives," which talks about the correlation between a person's level of education and staying out of prison. The article also relates the importance of educating prisoners and how, in California, doing so reduced the recidivism rate in the state by seven percent. At the time, a shockingly low number of incarcerated individuals in the state took academic or vocational courses.

The write-up also has information about the prominence of illiteracy among incarcerated individuals, but Louis could read and told me during our first interview that he liked to read books, especially the Bible. I'm not sure why I focused so much on illiteracy in that progress report, given that it wasn't an issue for Louis. Still, the overall point of incarcerated individuals not receiving the education they need was indeed an issue that pertained to my subject, and a topic Louis and I would delve into later.

On that first day together, Louis told me he was from Peoria and had a sister who was living and a brother who had died of lung cancer. He said he had a daughter and two sons, the second of whom was eighteen and had not seen Louis since he was six months old. Louis's voice turned defiant at times; that's how he sounded to me when he said his youngest son could track him down and see him sometime if he wanted to. Louis seemed like he wanted to visit with his youngest son and was regretful to have missed out on his life thus far. Apparently, his son's mother had kept Louis away from their child.

When I met him, Louis's life was on the upswing. He was staying at the ministry and working full time as a car detailer at Shield's Automotive in Rantoul. "I try to do my best at it, you know, get it back in tip-top shape," Louis said of the interiors and exteriors of the used cars he cleaned every day. Over the years, Louis's jobs had included pouring and finishing concrete, painting, laying carpet, and helping renovate houses.

As he described it to me, Louis's bureaucratic journey toward getting admitted into Jesus is the Way Prison Ministry didn't sound like an easy route. It also sounded as if the ministry was selective in whom it chooses. But Louis made the cut. He had been there for six months when I met him and liked it, not taking his residence at Jesus is the Way Ministry for granted. Along with volunteering at Books to Prisoners, Louis helped at The Salvation Army and at a food pantry in town, and he passed out food and water to homeless people in Champaign. "Some people like prayer," Louis said of the homeless individuals. "We pray for them."

As we wrapped up, Louis left me with these parting words: "I just thank God that I'm on the right track. You know, that I finally woke up and seen the light. That there's a better way than doing wrong. You know, that it's better to be on the other end, forget about myself sometimes and help others, which I always have did, either when I was in my addiction days and drinking, I did always have the will to want to help somebody, you know, so that's just natural with me, I guess. And, uh, just enjoy my life and get stronger in my faith."

The books Dash required us to read are worth mentioning because they so aptly conveyed what it means for a journalist to immerse himself into the thoughts, words, and actions of other people. Though the ethnographic study in the pages of *All Our Kin* took place in my own backyard of Champaign-Urbana, according to Dash, I had a hard time getting into that book. But I did get a lot out of *When Children Want Children: The Urban Crisis of Teenage Childbearing* (mentioned earlier in Dash's syllabus) and *Rosa Lee: A Mother and Her Family in Urban America*, both written by Dash.

What was fascinating to me as I read these books was *how* Dash attained the information he wrote about. As is written in the "Preface to the Illinois Paperback" section of *When Children Want Children*, Dash was astounded in the mid-1980s by the high rate of teenagers who were having babies in poor, urban locales in the U.S. He therefore spent a year in a rundown area of Washington, D.C., to try to find answers as to why it was happening. What he found out surprised him, and probably many readers were taken aback as well.

I respect how Dash pursued his topics and how he writes. I admire how he courageously inserted himself into the action of other people's lives for months on end. At the start of chapter three in *When Children Want Children*, he admits many folks didn't like him covering a topic he was curious about:

"Their reactions caused me to grow increasingly selective about the people with whom I shared my information or from whom I sought feedback," he wrote on page 57.

This is surprising, given how much we shared about people and their actions in his class. I was sorry to hear that Dash felt he couldn't comfortably relate with others on a topic he was passionate about. Here's what he wrote in the same paragraph:

"I found most middle-class professional people, white and black, opinionated, judgmental and antagonistic toward the people I was describing. Part of their reaction was linked to any open discussion of sexuality, an area of human behavior about which people have a host of hang-ups. I knew a number of my friends would not understand the need to write about teenage child-bearing among the black urban poor. I foresaw that many of the black middle class would be upset by this inquiry. They would feel vulnerable: tied to the behavior I would be describing. Their worries were justified because the larger, white society would identify the behavior of the underclass with them."

A few pages later, after mentioning that *some* people were interested in the topic he was pursuing, Dash wrote, "In other instances, I blundered, misjudging what the person's reaction would be. After a number of my approaches only angered people, I shared less and less of what I was grappling with fewer and fewer people. Most people were not even curious, and too many were offended by the details."

These are vulnerable thoughts by an esteemed former reporter from the *Washington Post*. If Dash can have doubts about what he was doing journalistically, I guess we're all allowed some uncertainties.

"I was reflecting on the number of people who didn't think that adolescent childbirth was worth looking at," Dash told me. "I saw it as a significant social crisis. Many other people didn't."

Dash said his in-depth coverage of adolescent pregnancy in an urban area also angered many black women, who felt a black male shouldn't be delving into such a topic. Dash said he didn't see any black women covering the topic, so he decided to examine it.

He dedicated his book *Rosa Lee* "to unfettered inquiry," fitting for a writer who spent four years following a troubled woman named Rosa Lee Cunningham, as well as her eight children and their many kids, in an effort to highlight a segment of the black underclass most never see. Dash related his thoughts on this journey in the Epilogue, writing in the first paragraph, "I became absorbed by Rosa Lee's story and deeply troubled by her choices—the ones she made and the ones she saw available to her."

Though *When Children Want Children* was mostly written in the third person, Dash said he "went all out" with including his personal observations in *Rosa Lee*. Some of the anger Dash had over Rosa Lee's family issues caused him to at times get angry and pull back from her.

One day during the writing of *Rosa Lee,* Dash had a bad headache that was made worse by Rosa Lee's decision to tell two of her children about a $1,600 disability check he knew they would hound her for to satiate their drug habit. Dash knew he would have to hear about it from Rosa Lee, who had HIV and genuinely needed the money. His anger over this situation was further etched into his memory when he picked up on a noticeable change in his voice that he heard while transcribing the book.

"She didn't pick it up," Dash said, "but I could hear my voice go from reporter to the angry Leon Dash. I wasn't expressing the anger, but I could hear the change in my voice when she had told me something, and it angered me."

Dash later apologized to Rosa Lee for blowing up at her. Rosa Lee, however, didn't even realize the reporter was mad. In fact, she said Dash's response made her feel good because no one else cared enough about her to monitor her dire financial situation.

As the semester went on, I would see what Dash meant by becoming engrossed with the subject you were writing about. And I became aware of the disturbing options and patterns that some people in life are born into and then fall into.

For our first in-depth interview, the one about Louis's time in school, we met at Jesus is the Way Ministry. The room we talked in had the vibe of a classroom, with rows of desks and computers surrounding us. Our subsequent interviews would take place in fast-food joints, which I think appealed to Louis more. He told me it was nice to leave the building when he could. I think the simple, non-ministry-related activity of eating and talking at McDonald's for a few hours was a nice getaway for him.

Amazingly, Louis had memories of skipping school as far back as kindergarten, hanging out with his older stepsister, Sally, and her friends. He didn't even know what skipping out on school meant, but he did know that at times he wasn't at school when he should have been. The kids' grandmother found out what was going on and, according to Louis, "whooped us 'cause we were supposed to be in school."

Years later, in fifth grade, Louis said he started smoking weed in rolled-up newspaper. Like his days of not knowing what skipping classes even entailed, he didn't know what "getting high" was. Louis said he received his fair share of paddle whacks that year from his teacher, who would strike the children for offenses such as saying "shut up."

Louis said he was slugging beers during these early years of his life, as well. His mom and stepdad often traveled the country (more on that later), so Sally was left to raise him as best she could. Louis didn't listen to his stepsister much and began skipping school a lot more to hang out at a friend's house and hit the pool hall. His mom and stepdad sent their kids letters from the road.

Louis's teacher in sixth grade, obviously upset by something Louis said or did, once pulled him from his chair and threw him against a wall, hurting the child's back. At that tender age, Louis said he gave up on school.

The story gets sadder. Since no one else could apparently do it, Louis was forced to take care of his mom, who had lupus. His schooling, which didn't sound great to begin with, devolved into nothing more than a man coming by the house with pamphlets, going over a problem or two and dishing out reading assignments. This is the way Louis remembered it, anyway.

Following his mom's death, Louis continued his schooling but never received a high school diploma. He did take some educational courses in prison, where he said his spelling improved. To pass the time while incarcerated, Louis began reading biographies and writing his daughter. For all his troubles, he knew the importance of an education and wanted to further his knowledge, even after getting out of prison. "I'm gonna get my GED one day," he told me. "I'm gonna get it."

Since there were only six students in Dash's class, you really got to know about the interviewees and the intricacies of their lives. I told my classmates everything I discovered about Louis, and they in turn openly told the class what they were learning.

I don't recall whom the Asian girl who sat to the left of me was writing about, unfortunately. I do remember she was a cheery person who was always smiling and laughing. To the right of me was a dark-haired female student whose interviewee was even more troubled than mine, and that's saying a lot. I abided by Dash's rule to not judge and be as unbiassed as possible, but it was hard sometimes to not be shocked by the travails, many of them self-inflicted, that some people go through.

A black student named Reggie sat at the end of the table, on the opposite side of Dash. He was a good-humored guy who was studying to be a lawyer and in his final semester, with plans to move to Los Angeles after graduating. When the class concluded, Reggie told everyone he was grateful to the University of Illinois for offering an Immersion Journalism course, a classy thing to say. Lawyers and paralegals often interview their clients extensively, and Dash's course no doubt helped prepare Reggie to do that.

Reggie's subject was a retired scholar who sounded rather dull compared to what others of us were talking about in class. The biggest thing about this guy was that he'd never married or had children, so there was speculation that he was an asexual person. Reggie informed us that his subject had had a few relationships in the past but had simply never wanted to marry. Broaching this topic with his interviewee was difficult for Reggie, I think.

A black female student sat on the opposite side of the table from me, and I don't recall the person she interviewed. The black student to the right of her, Augustus Wood, was an activist for racial justice causes. Years later I learned that Wood was the host of a campus podcast called Off the Shelf, a show in which he talks to black scholars who discuss noteworthy books.

During the final minutes of the last day of class, Dash wanted to take a group photo of all of us, with him in it. He must have had a timer on his camera or phone and perhaps a tripod, or maybe someone came into the classroom to take the picture. In the image, Wood and the Asian girl are on the left, and I'm third from the right next to Dash, who has his arm around my shoulder. The dark-haired female student is standing to the right of Dash, and next to her is the black female student and then Reggie. We're all smiling, probably relieved to be done with a tough but rewarding course, which began in August with so many more students in it. Except for Dash, I've never seen any of these people again. Nonetheless, it's one of my most cherished photos.

For our next three interviews, Louis and I went to Hardees twice and McDonald's once. In retrospect, I'm not sure these public places were the best spots to talk to my Immersion Journalism subject, given that we were covering such personal topics and I needed to learn a lot. Perhaps a quieter room where we could be alone, such as where we'd had our first in-depth interview, might have been more appropriate and would have made me feel a little less self-conscious at times. When I later played back some of the tapes, I could hear the softness in my voice as I asked Louis certain questions, conscious of the fact that the couple eating cheeseburgers next to us might be eavesdropping as I inquired about personal aspects of Louis's life.

But Louis was comfortable in these joints, and he had no hesitation revealing a lot about his life to me. I always paid for his meals, not because I felt sorry for his current circumstances—I actually thought he was being well taken care of at Jesus is the Way Ministry—but because he was nice enough to take the time to talk to me for a significant number of hours on subjects that often did not put him in the finest light.

The second in-depth interview about Louis growing up in his family began in a depressing way, with him telling me his father died when his car "ran up under a semitruck" and he broke his neck. The lady in the car with him, not Louis's mom, was lucky to only suffer a broken arm, according to Louis. Louis's memories of his father while growing up in Peoria, Illinois, were not great.

"They say he was really mean," Louis said of his dad. "He was mean towards my mom. He liked to fight her all the time. Every picture I see of him, he's in the nightclub."

Later, after moving to Battle Creek, Michigan, when he was around 11 years old, Louis had a stepdad who pushed him against a wall and hurt his back (like what his sixth grade teacher apparently did to him). Louis said his brother witnessed this and grabbed a .22 pistol, threatening to kill their stepdad, who never roughed up Louis again after that.

But his musician stepdad, Ray Freeman, was gone most of the time anyway, often out on tour with Junior Walker and the All Stars, the 1960s Motown group. Walker sang and played the saxophone, and Louis's stepdad played guitar—Louis said he sounded like George Benson. Junior Walker's band had a slew of hits, the most well-known of which might be "Shotgun."

Louis's brother had a fascination with guns and got into his share of trouble growing up. The two had fistfights often, Louis said. On the calmer side of things, his sister liked to sew and would make her own clothes. Despite the turmoil in his life, Louis's time in Battle Creek had its idyllic moments.

"We had a nice house," he told me. "We stayed in a nice neighborhood. It was blacks and whites. We had a two-story house. We had a real big old garage. It was like a barn. We had a big old long driveway. My stepdad made good money."

Ray was into CB radios and sounded like a technically gifted guy, according to the accounts of Louis, who said he would build his own amplifiers and rebuild CBs and ham radios. A "big ol' antenna" stuck up from the family's roof, and sometimes Louis would help Ray with it.

"Ray taught me how to use tools," he said. "That's how I picked up using tools, 'cause we had tools, and I would use them [to] fix my bike. And I be out there watchin' him work on cars. I know what to hand him, you know, while he up under the car."

Louis said he visited Junior Walker's "big old mansion" on a hill every weekend when the musician was in town. He recalls several German shepherds running around, nice cars everywhere, and a swimming pool that was shaped like a saxophone. "I used to talk to Junior Walker all the time," Louis said. "He was just normal."

Despite being exposed to some of the finer things in life through a popular musician, Louis drifted toward darker, illicit actions. He often rode his bike around with friends, a normal childhood activity, but also smoked marijuana. He once tried on a pair of shoes in a store, with his mom right there, and knowingly walked out of the place, trying to take them without paying. His mom was reprimanded for Louis's act, so he stopped trying to steal—at least for a while.

"But as I got older, that's what I started going to prison for—shoplifting," Louis said. "After my mom passed away, I just didn't care ... 'bout nothin'. I was missing her, and I feel I didn't have nobody, so I didn't care if they locked me up."

Along with taking a midterm exam, we had to turn in a mid-semester story on the subjects we were writing about. My midterm paper is dated October 15, 2014, and has the rather newsy title "Caretaking boy escapes education, turns to life of crime." I'm not sure now why I chose the word "escapes" to describe how Louis ducked his formal education in life—it's not the most accurate word to relate how his life was. Louis didn't "escape" his education, as if he were on the run from some teacher who was eager to educate him. The reality, at least from what I could gather during my interviews, is that Louis's spotty record as a student is more the result of a lack of parental supervision, a lack of caring on his part, perhaps a bad school system, and a depressing turn when his mom got sick, since Louis was the primary family member who looked out for her.

Though the title of the story wasn't perfect, I submitted it for publication a few months later to Smile Politely, without Dash knowing, and it was published. The title in the Smile Politely version reads "Caretaking person" instead of "Caretaking boy." Here's how the piece begins:

When Louis Postlewaite, Jr., was around ten years old, he was privy to the sounds of a well-known Motown band rehearsing on the "big ol'" front porch of his family's house in Battle Creek, Michigan. Sometimes he would even record the lively music played by Junior Walker and the All-Stars on his reel-to-reel tape, shyly listening for mistakes by the professional musicians.

The boy had an all-access pass to Battle Creek native Junior Walker and his cohorts thanks to his stepdad, Edmund "Ray" R. Freeman, who, according to his 2011 obituary in the Peoria Journal Star, was a "unique guitarist" who toured and played with the likes of Walker, Wes Montgomery, the Bill Doggett Combo, and numerous other artists. Many years later, at the age of fifty-eight, Postlewaite said his stepfather's licks reminded him of George Benson's.

But his reel-to-reels are long gone, and the music-filled memories that Postlewaite recalled on his porch during the mid-1960s have faded. Behind the music, Postlewaite and his siblings—an older sister and a younger brother—were largely unsupervised. While his parents went out on tour for weeks with the Junior Walker ensemble, leaving $200 on the TV set in their wake, the children fended for themselves. His sister was in charge when Ray and Mom were gone, but that was laughable.

"I wouldn't never listen to her," Postlewaite said.

Here's the heart of the piece:

Postlewaite's life changed drastically when his mom became sick with lupus, a chronic, autoimmune disease that damages the body and can last for years. The Battle Creek kid who built go-carts, rode his bike everywhere with friends, and occasionally went horseback riding suddenly found himself as the main caretaker for his slowly dying mom. Postlewaite and his mother moved in with his mom's grandparents in Peoria, where he was born. His siblings stayed in Michigan, while Ray, who would end up marrying four other women, fled the family. The danceable sounds and searing saxophone solos of Junior Walker were already long in the past.

"I wanted to do a lot of things until my mom got sick," Postlewaite said. *"Because I took care of her. That's why I stopped going to school. I took care of my mom."*

When he should have been attending the seventh grade, Postlewaite bathed his mother, read to her, and cleaned her bed sores. He changed her catheter and combed her hair. His grandparents were around to help, but their assistance was limited since they worked. Much of the woman's care fell on the boy's shoulders.

"She couldn't walk," he said. *"I had to put her in the tub. She had lost all her weight. She never smoked or cussed or none of that. But God would give me enough strength to help her get in the tub and get out."*

But a higher power did not take care of Postlewaite's education as he fell further and further behind. His schooling by this point had devolved to a tutor stopping by the house twice a week for brisk and breezy lessons. He gave the student some pamphlets, helped him work on a problem or two, and dispensed a reading assignment.

Not that Postlewaite, or even his mom, cared about the missed schooling. Nothing was ever said about the boy's education. He skipped school half the time prior to his mom's sickness anyway, and a more important goal had been established.

"I just wanted to help get my mom get well. That was my main concern," he said.

That didn't happen. His mom perished when he was sixteen, and Postlewaite's life took a turn for the worse. The tested youth had dropped out of school, but he showed fortitude in attempting to help and comfort his mother. All that bravery went out the window when she died.

Louis Postlewaite gave up on life for a long time after the death of Norma Jean Sanders, succumbing to drugs, alcohol, and illicit behavior.

The picture I took of Louis at the top of the Smile Politely piece shows a sad, tired-looking man wearing a white sweatshirt, as the straw from his soft drink pokes up from the bottom of the image. A Houdini poster and various pictures on the wall behind Louis somewhat liven up the background of the everyday fast-food restaurant. A lamp hangs and empty tables await possible late-night customers besides us. There's a concerned, sort of searching look in Louis's expression. He held nothing back in our interviews, and I think he appreciated me taking the time to tell his life story.

God was a focal point of the reformed Louis's life during the time I knew him, and a higher power was not a foreign concept to him prior to that period. He'd been raised as a churchgoing child in Peoria. But by the time Louis moved to Michigan in his youth, the regular family church excursions had ceased. Still, religion continued to weave its way into Louis's life in varied ways, even during the worst of times, and even if it meant stumbling into church while blazing drunk with people shushing him.

Louis's Uncle William, his dad's brother, had been a Baptist preacher and had tried sometimes to instill what was right and what was wrong into his nephew. Louis said his uncle was a low-key pastor who preached straight from the Bible. Later, when Louis started going to prison on a regular basis, William would write him regularly, which Louis appreciated.

Church and fellowship were big parts of Louis's life when I was interviewing him; he was meeting a lot of people at the church he attended in Rantoul and liked the atmosphere. When I asked Louis if he had ever turned his back on God, he told me emphatically that he had several times, and that prison had been the result after every negligent period toward his faith.

"Things would look good for me, and, uh, I'd just end up back out in the streets," Louis said. "Meet the wrong girl; we start doin' drugs again and right back on the same boat. And forget what God got me; God got me that job, you know, got me in a good place, and I just blow it."

Louis said there were numerous times when he could have overdosed on cocaine and crack cocaine—especially one time in particular—but that God kept him around for a reason. I wondered if that reason was to clean up his life in Rantoul to help others turn their lives around.

Our third in-depth interview went into topics of conflict and mayhem in Louis's life, but one brief line of questioning caught my eye as I read the transcript years later, perhaps because of its refreshing innocence: I asked Louis, who had never married, if there was a special lady he had his eye on. He said he knew a woman who lived in Champaign named Gwynn, whom he wanted to ask out on a date but couldn't since dating wasn't allowed at Jesus is the Way Ministry. Louis said she was somewhat of a churchgoing woman, and he had plans to make her a full-time one after he left Jesus is the Way Ministry.

"I'd like to get married one day," he said. "I'd like to get married to a church girl. I asked God to send me one. Send me a wife."

Following our interviews, Dash had us do a valuable exercise in which we reviewed our transcripts and created "self-critique" questions that we neglected to ask our subjects but could inquire about during the next interview. Doing this helped us examine our conversations and think deeply about how we could better get to know our interviewees the next time around.

Dash said he did the same thing as a reporter because he would sometimes realize while transcribing interviews that he had left out an important question or two.

"I would make a note to myself, the next time you see this person, you need to get this question answered," he said. "This is a hole here, a hole in the story. And before you sit down and write, you have to fill in all the holes. And I know students, doing this for the first time, don't have that kind of perspective or discipline to examine what they've done and think they've got it all."

Here are the self-critique questions I neglected to ask Louis during our third in-depth interview, all of which I asked him when we next met:

- Do you think if you'd stayed in Peoria and gone to church on a regular basis with your grandmother that you would have avoided a life of crime later on?
- Do you think your dad and brother, who was a preacher and family man, were radically different people, and if so, why?
- When you were a kid in Peoria, why didn't you go to the Baptist church that your uncle preached at?
- What did your uncle say to you in his letters that he sent you when you were in prison?
- When Rick Shields in Rantoul gave you a job, what did he say about your troubled past and his expectations from you at work?
- You mentioned the chemicals you have to breathe in when you work indoors at Shields Auto. Can you tell me more about that?
- I sense that you take a lot of pride in your job at Shields. Why is that?
- Tell me more about meeting the wrong girls in your life who have steered you toward the wrong path. Did that happen a lot to you? Have you had a lot of girlfriends in your life?
- Have you ever been homeless?
- Have you ever sold drugs?
- Tell me about the episode when you had a heart attack. What age were you?

-   How scared were you in prison and why? You mentioned you got things from your friends in prison. What sorts of things were they?

Looking back, I realize now I also neglected to inquire about what may have also been a highly relevant issue in Louis's life: racism. I *think* that I did broach this topic in our first in-depth interview, with him brushing it off, saying that he alone was responsible for many of his hardships. Yet I should have pursued the subject more persistently, as Dash advised in his syllabus. I have a feeling if I would have asked about racism in different ways throughout our time together, Louis would have given me valuable information to better round out his story. It was a big oversight on my part.

At this point I had interviewed Louis four times, and the sheets of transcribed paper were beginning to add up to a sizable stack on my desk. My first in-depth talk with Louis resulted in 40 pages and 13,766 words of transcribed material; the second one had me typing out 49 pages and 16,894 words; and the third interview led to 33 pages and 11,998 words. I was learning tons about Louis and had a mountain of paper to prove it.

Transcribing was such a huge part of Dash's class that I had no choice but to do the mundane task during a weekend getaway to Saugatuck, Michigan, early on in the semester with my wife and Logan and several family members on my wife's side. While everyone else spent their Saturday having a blast riding on sandy dunes and on a duck boat, I was in a drab upstairs bedroom of the house we were staying at, standing in front of the very laptop I'm writing on now, listening to my voice and Louis's on a recorder, typing out every single word. I had no choice: if I didn't transcribe, I would fall behind in the class. Dash wanted the highlights of all the talks. To find those golden nuggets of conversation, I had to listen to and write out every word that was said.

All that transcribing convinced me that as tempting as it may be for storytellers to pay to have their recordings transcribed by someone else, there is no substitute for doing the work yourself. By listening to the conversation again and typing it all out, you *truly* begin to know your subject and can begin to formulate a story in your mind.

One day, I noticed one of the interview sessions within the stack of papers on my desk was missing. After some sleuthing, I discovered that my wife, Jill, had spotted the transcripts in my office and was reading them—voraciously.

"He had been through a lot," Jill told me years later, as I was writing this book, "so he had a good story to tell, and he was willing to share it."

Jill doesn't recall now what she was so riveted by regarding Louis's life, but she said the transcripts got better and more revealing as time went on.

"I think he was honest, and I think that just came with meeting with you multiple times," she said.

I was secretly pleased she was so entertained by Louis's life. It made all the transcribing I was doing feel like it was more worth the effort.

The final interview I conducted with Louis, which covered his life outside the family he grew up in, demonstrates the importance of journalists asking good questions, follow-ups to those questions, and throwing in what may seem like innocuous inquiries to see where they may lead.

The interview was humming along in no particular direction as we reviewed topics we'd covered before such as Louis's church life and his current job in Rantoul. He worked for Rick Shields at Shields Auto Center, a position he attained by persistently trying to get a hold of Rick Shields after submitting his work application.

"If I wouldn't have went up there, I'd a still be waitin' on him to call me," Louis said. "But he had good thoughts 'cause he had my application right there. I see him every day at work."

The interview got interesting when he started talking to me about the dangers of his drug use and prison life. Louis didn't have any scary stories to relate about prison—mostly he kept to himself, though he did make some good friends during his incarcerations. He was telling me about how some facilities were better than others in terms of the vibe he felt from other prisoners. The facility in East Moline, he said, was rougher than the correctional center in Shawnee, where Louis was locked up at for close to five years.

All this prison talk must have made me ask Louis how he got the scar on his cheek. In retrospect, it's hard to believe I didn't ask him about his scar much earlier, but I'm glad I brought it up. Here is what he said:

This girl cut me. She threw a ashtray at me. 'Cause I wouldn't give her no drugs. We were gettin' high together, and I wouldn't give her no more dope. And she got mad and … the inside of the ashtray cut me.
What kind of drugs?
She wanted crack-cocaine.
When did this happen?
It been a while. It been like 15 years ago. Probably longer than that.
What did you do after she threw it and cut you?
I left. I had met this older guy. I used to pay him to come there and get high, you know, when I didn't want to be bothered with people, I would go there. I went there. The police found me from the blood drip. I try to burn her house down. I set her porch on fire. You know, I told 'em I'm gonna kill everyone in the house. I set her porch on fire with some lighter fluid. And the police found me from the blood. They found the blood trail; that's how they found me.
Did you get in trouble for that?
No.
Why?
She didn't never press charges and say that I did it.
What would have happened if she did?
Probably try to get me for arson. That's like thirty years.
Why didn't she press charges?
I don't know. She still liked me. She just was bad on drugs.
Do you have other scars?
Yeah. Got a scar right there [points to his upper chest].
How'd you get it?
My kids' momma stabbed me.
Why?
I used to have a bad habit every Friday. We was young then. I think we was like 21 when she stabbed me. Twenty-one or twenty-two. I would get paid and didn't want to give her no money, help her with the bills and nothin'. And I kept my clothes at the cleaners, and I'd go get my clothes out the cleaners, and I'm funna go to Chicago or somewhere for the weekend. And she got tired of that. We got to arguin' and I was callin' out her name and she walked up to me and stuck me with a steak knife.
Did you have to go to the hospital?
Nope, I went upstairs and wrapped myself, put a towel around me and got into bed. So, she ended up comin' gettin' in the bed later on that night.
And it just healed up okay?
Yep, I let it heal. I was workin' at this junkyard and they noticed that it, uh, I had some overalls on. Blood was, it started bleedin' and they sent me home. But I never went to the hospital for it.
What did you say or do to her afterward?

Well, I knocked her teeth out. When I got up that morning to go to work, she was sleepin', and I hit her in the mouth with my fist.

Is that the only time you've ever hit a girlfriend?

Uh, me and her used to fight all the time. Me and my kids' momma used to fight all the time. That's Tenille and Louis mom.

What's her name?

Brenda.

Have you been violent any other times with women?

No, just her.

This exchange paints a bad picture of Louis, the worst he conveyed to me during our talks. But beyond this troubled side of Louis, I also discovered a man who strongly believed in God and was trying hard to redeem himself by assisting others. When I wrote my final fifteen-page story on Louis in Dash's class, I titled it "The Man Who Lives to Help" and covered his good and not-so-good qualities, characteristics we are all blessed and cursed with. That story was the third-place winner of the Marian and Barney Brody Creative Feature Article Writing Award in Journalism in the College of Media at Illinois. The thrill of earning $1,000 for winning and being recognized at the 2015 College of Media Honors Reception by none other than Professor Rich Martin in a roomful of faculty, students, parents, and alumni of the college was something I'll never forget.

The last time I ever saw Louis was in December of 2014, not long after our final interview together. He was volunteering for Jesus is the Way Ministry at Virginia Theatre in Champaign. Jill, Logan, and I had just watched a show and were heading out of the building among the bustling crowd. Logan got to see Louis for a second time, and it was Jill's first time meeting him. It was close to Christmas and there was a jubilant feeling in the air. Louis had been such a big part of my life for several months, so I was glad I had run into him with my family.

Less than two years later he was dead, and I don't know how he passed. I will forever be grateful to Louis for his willingness to talk so openly and simply be himself with no pretentions or guile. We should all be so brave.

Chapter 4: Jarvis Journalism, Studious Thoughts, and Tough Guy's Insights

Changes were afoot as I plowed on in the program. To this point, my classes had mostly been hands-on learning experiences. I was going out into the world and meeting people, talking to men and women about subjects I never would have otherwise, and then writing about these individuals and what they did in the most factual, interesting way I could. I was putting into real-world practice the journalistic advice I got from professors who had remarkable backgrounds, people who had won awards and written books and edited for newspapers and had been in the reporting trenches for decades. In addition, I'd taken an editing class that had pushed me to the limit to eke out an A-. These courses had been challenging, but I was getting so much out of them. Now, I was apprehensive about what came next.

That's because I wasn't exactly sure what *did* come next. Compared to the hands-on reporting I'd done in my other classes so far, the Issues in Journalism course I was about to take sounded like a more esoteric version of journalism, an area of the craft I was curious about and certainly wanted to master, but also a realm that I was ... a bit unsure of. Here's a short description of the class:

"Seminar on issues of contemporary importance in journalism in their historical, multicultural contexts. Emphasis on ethical, legal, social, professional aspects of those issues. Aimed at helping students develop their own journalism philosophies and high standards of conduct."

The course was taught by Matt Ehrlich, who has emeritus status at the university. During his tenure at Illinois, Ehrlich won the Campus Award for Excellence in Undergraduate Teaching. His background in journalism is rich with varied work in reporting, editing, producing, and working as an anchor at WILL in Urbana. He has written books focusing on journalism in popular culture and one about the relationships between cities and sports, *Kansas City vs. Oakland: The Bitter Sports Rivalry That Defined an Era*. His research about the history of news stories on animals, specifically cats, and why that realm of news is important to critique, was publicized at the university while I was taking his course. Later, in 2021, Ehrlich released the book *Dangerous Ideas on Campus: Sex, Conspiracy, and Academic Freedom in the Age of JFK*. He retired in the summer of 2016 but continues to teach courses at Illinois.

"Being retired, I feel like I have a little bit more flexibility as to what to write about," Ehrlich told me. "I'm not always having to focus so much on journalism per se, although journalism does play a role in this latest book, especially the DI [*The Daily Illini*] because it looks at how students were living through these events and becoming more politically aware at a time when Roger Ebert was the editor-in-chief at the DI back in '63, '64."

Professor Ehrlich's manner reminded me of a session moderator, in a class that leaned heavily on group discussions. Like me, he grew up in an era when daily printed newspapers provided many with the news of the day. Ehrlich read them daily and would swap sections of the paper around the table with his family. Times have changed, though. I remember Professor Ehrlich once showing the class a front-page article from a major newspaper with news published that day, information that was already dated since further developments of the story had occurred and were online.

Ehrlich was engaging during our phone conversation five years after I took his course. He was happy to talk about the current state of journalism and genuinely interested in the book I was working on, jokingly hoping it wasn't an "expose" on the journalism department at Illinois. He mentioned to me a few newspapers he subscribes to these days, and I couldn't resist asking him if he received the print or online versions. Perhaps the retired scholar still swapped sections of the printed newspaper with loved ones over a steaming cup of coffee on the kitchen counter.

"I do the digital subscriptions," Ehrlich said. "It's been a long time since I picked up a print newspaper."

"How come?" I asked.

"It's more convenient. I think I actually consume more news since I started doing digital media. Now, this is not a huge concern, but environmentally, I think it's better not to have the print product, and not to subscribe to the print product and then need to recycle. I mean, I know that you do lose some things, probably, in terms of the serendipity of your eye running across something that you might not otherwise see on the digital version. Sometimes I will just glance at the latest updates, whereas with the print newspaper it was more likely that I would actually spend more time looking at each page of the newspaper, even if I was just scanning each page of the newspaper briefly. So, yeah, I think you do lose some things, but especially for convenience, always being able to check things on my phone, not having to dispose of a physical product afterward, I just find it more congenial."

For the second semester in a row, I'd be learning in the atmosphere of Room 336. On the one hand, the room was the same: the long wood table, the floral-patterned rug, the wood paneling, and the projector from the ceiling were all still there. But the people were different, as was the class content, which somehow made the room feel new and unfamiliar. It was hard to imagine repeating the stimulation I felt as we went around the table in Leon Dash's class, talking about our interview subjects in what felt like our own private bubble of journalistic experiences, with Dash asking probing questions. Professor Ehrlich's class didn't have a ton of students, but there were more in his class than in Dash's. For the first time since starting the graduate program, I felt an inexplicable wave of hesitation, as if I didn't belong.

But I had to get over that feeling, and fast. Issues in Journalism was an important course that got to the heart of what ethical journalism is, while taking into consideration how the field has had to evolve, from a business standpoint, to keep up with the times. After reading the syllabus, I saw it was a less obscure version of journalism than I had originally thought. Here's an excerpt:

"We also will look broadly at the principles, forms, audiences and business models of today's U.S. journalism, including debates involving journalistic transparency, curation, mobile news, data journalism, digital innovation, automation, niche journalism, content marketing, paywalls, crowdfunding, web analytics and nonprofit news. The exact issues and case studies we will examine may change depending on current events."

The thrust of Issues in Journalism came down to two separate books, which we were required to write about extensively: *The Elements of Journalism: What Newspeople Should Know and the Public Should Expect* by Bill Kovach and Tom Rosenstiel; and *Geeks Bearing Gifts* by Jeff Jarvis, which was based on essays he had published. When I think of these books now,

Elements of Journalism calls to mind the Walter Cronkite version of journalism that strives for truthfulness in the most forthright—perhaps even staid, some might say—way. *Geeks Bearing Gifts* aims to shake up the world of journalism without apology.

Professor Ehrlich agreed with my general assessment of the two "backbone" books of the course, saying, "They do portray contrasting viewpoints as to what journalism should be and where journalism should go, as of 2015." He was quick to add that 2015 was eons ago in the ever-changing world of journalism; please remember that while reading on.

Ehrlich said Jarvis was good at provoking thought in an exceedingly conscious way. "He's adopted that provocateur approach consistently as an educator. And for a class like [Issues in Journalism], I thought it was a very useful tool."

The Elements of Journalism by Kovach and Rosenstiel is undoubtedly inspiring if you care about news in a knowledgeable and informed democratic society. In my view, journalism by trained professionals should *always* hold itself to the high ideals talked about in the authors' book. Similar high principles are covered in the Society of Professional Journalists' Code of Ethics document, which we covered in Ehrlich's class. This piece emphasizes the importance of reporting the truth, minimizing harm to subjects, acting independently, and always being transparent.

With the industry in flux on various fronts, both when I was in graduate school and now, Kovach and Rosenstiel convey in their book several journalistic principles that can help today's reporters remain above the fray of unsubstantiated or untruthful news stories. More than ever, news readers need on-the-spot reporters who can verify reliable information and make sense of events while putting everything in fair context. Kovach and Rosenstiel believe citizens deserve principled journalists who can responsibly curate information, empower readers, build communities, and act as role models for a public that has for years been understandably leery of published news.

At the same time, the way people receive their news has changed drastically since the digital era began. More radical thinkers in the industry, such as Jeff Jarvis, who is an author, professor, and blogger, advocate for wholesale changes in journalism, using the fruits of whiz-bang technology to enhance the field. And some of his suggestions, however brazenly related, have merit.

"It's about turning journalism on its head and listening to the communities that we serve and first find out what their needs are," Jarvis told an audience at the September 25, 2014, Online News Association Conference in Chicago.

Some of Jarvis's objectives, such as better informing society, are aligned with those of Kovach and Rosenstiel, though the ways to achieve such goals are different. To accomplish the shared goal of enlightening the public in today's world, it's reasonable to say that journalists can take rational approaches to both live up to the standards shown in *The Elements of Journalism* and implement some of the worthwhile suggestions advocated by Jarvis.

Kovach and Rosenstiel are aware of the digital transformations in today's world of journalism, and they embrace the platforms in which news can be transmitted. In this environment, both budding journalists and veteran newspaper men and women should keep Kovach and Rosenstiel's values at the forefront.

In the "Engagement, Collaboration, and Membership" chapter of his book *Geeks Bearing Gifts*, Jarvis laments society's apathy toward news organizations today, as well as young people's declining interest in the news. Yet a platform in which young people *are* getting their news more often in recent years is on mobile devices, according to the article "Unlocking mobile revenue and audience: New ideas and best practices" by Jeff Sonderman.

As it came to prominence, the mobile platform offered hope to the business side of news, though generating revenue through mobile ads was more complex than typical advertising methods of the past. Sonderman's article describes a 2014 American Press Institute Thought

Leader Summit in which journalism experts in mobile technology gathered to talk shop. In a section of the piece titled "Editorial technology and business teams must work together," the writer says that unlike the "older days," the newsroom, sales team, and IT department must collaborate.

"Mobile, like online technology in general, ties revenue more directly to content, and content more directly to technology," Sonderman writes. "The people responsible for all three parts of an organization have to work together."

Ehrlich hasn't kept up with the newer business models or experiments of today's media since retiring, but he reiterated some of the thoughts he touched on in our class.

"Subscription-based models, foundation-based models, media being owned by the equivalent of Jeff Bezos, I think there's always a tradeoff with concerns about potential political interference when those things happen, but again, that's nothing new," Ehrlich said. "The most important thing is to have a secure source of funding along with some pledge of non-editorial interference coming from ownership."

Ehrlich mentioned local journalism as an area that particularly needs a supportable financial model for the benefit of society. After all, what will be the viable alternative if too many "news deserts" nationwide—communities where local print news is not readily available—take hold?

Penelope Muse Abernathy, the Knight Chair in Journalism and Digital Media Economics at the University of North Carolina (UNC), has some recommendations in this area—so many, in fact, that she wrote a book about the topic. It was one of the optional reads we had in Ehrlich's class.

I recall what my dad said to me one day as I sat at the dining room table, hunched over a *USA Today* newspaper. He told me I was "the last of a dying breed," someone who still reads newspapers. My dad—more than two decades older than me—said this to me in *1996*.

The surging digital world of the mid-1990s would soon change the lives of everyone in numerous ways, but legacy media seemed so permanent and safe at the time, at least to me. My dad, a savvy businessman, had a premonition that the world would change.

And did it ever change. *Saving Community Journalism: The Path to Profitability*, written by Penelope Muse Abernathy, has a quaint-sounding title and a clever cover showing newspaper vending machines encased within the four walls of a tablet device. The implication is clear: how people have gotten their news since 1996 has changed drastically.

For "dying-breed" folks like me, Abernathy's book offers hope, though the path to sustaining quality journalism on a local level requires innovations. The findings in her book were the result of extensive research, including approximately five years of "in-field strategy work" with the help of nearly 200 students in the School of Journalism and Mass Communications at UNC. The three sections of Abernathy's book cover how community newspapers can develop strategies to deal with a changing readership and environment; how they must concentrate on organizational and operational challenges; and how transformative technology has affected the newspaper environment.

The author takes an expansive view of community newspapers, choosing not to focus on circulation numbers, and instead concentrating on the missions and markets of several papers in the U.S. that have a readership range of 7,000 to 150,000.

To bolster her ideas, Abernathy and her team developed accompanying websites at businessofnews.unc.edu (now defunct) and savingcommunityjournalism.com, both of which were designed for publishers and editors of community newspapers as well as start-up nonprofit organizations.

Complementing her book with online material was a savvy and apt move by the author, considering the heavy focus in *Saving Community Journalism* of a strategized print-online plan that she recommends newspapers employ. My hope while reading Abernathy's book was that newspapers—in the print form I have always cherished—could thrive with astute business decisions, updated content that wowed the world, and a bit of luck. The reality, according to Abernathy, is that digital media has taken over and print newspapers have a short time frame to implement bolder print-web alliances that involve both content and advertising—or else.

Printed newspapers still drew more readers and garnered bigger advertising profits than their accompanying websites when Abernathy's book was published. But things are different now. The year 2015, when I was taking Ehrlich's class, now seems like 1996 in terms of where advertising dollars are going (hint: not as much to newspapers). Fewer people are hunched over dining room tables reading a printed version of the newspaper (like I did) or exchanging sections of the paper to family members (like Ehrlich did).

Abernathy's book offers both practical and innovative ideas for newspaper executives, editors, writers, and those in advertising. The practices of several papers are brought to light, both their mistakes and successes, pulling readers into certain newsroom quandaries, some of which were still being sorted out at the time of the writing. What is emphasized continually is that what works successfully in one newspaper market may not work in another. Newspapers featured in the book, such as *The Whiteville News Reporter* in North Carolina, *La Raza* in Chicago, and the *Naples Daily News*, each have their own problems and success stories. What pans out and doesn't pan out varies by region and readership.

The *Dallas Morning News*, for example, experimented with an "unbundling" model of the paper, in which readers pay to access and view proprietary information put out by the publication such as calendar events and sports news.

One portion of the book relates how the *Whiteville News Reporter* established four community pages online and in print, content that supplemented and enhanced both media forms in different ways. The pages were labeled Curious Citizens, Sports of All Sorts, Front Porch Neighbors, and Plugged-In Parents. The sports community page was a huge hit online, according to Abernathy. Unfortunately, the paper struggled with the limited manpower it had to produce the other three sponsored sections. Only the sports community page was accessible when I last checked the paper's website.

Another nugget of repeated advice in *Saving Community Journalism*, directed at newspaper editors and publishers, is to cut costs annually by a rate of six percent for five years, whittling down expenses by thirty percent. It is expensive to create, print, and distribute thousands of printed newspapers. For many, shedding legacy costs involves cutting back on delivery, consolidating business functions, creating hybrid positions, outsourcing the printing of the paper, and working in a cloud environment.

Sadly, the thirty percent cost reduction in five years' time still may not be enough to save many local newspapers. As folks flee the industry, you can't help but notice in the book the number of *former* journalists who offer their thoughts, people who are now either scholars teaching journalism or who are in entirely different industries.

Abernathy says newspaper ad reps need to make the change from being mere order takers for classified ads to becoming marketing experts who can confidently recommend to a business how to advertise on multiple print and digital platforms in a targeted way. Current graduate students in journalism, as well as those working in the field, may find this information and other advice in the book to be obvious by now. But that doesn't make *Saving Community Journalism* any less important; much of what is said in the book is still pertinent to everyday citizens who also have a big stake in the future of their community newspapers. The book offers hope and a call for rewired thinking, making clear that a one-size-fits-all approach is not going to solve journalism's dilemmas.

Journalists are trained to be skeptical, rightly so, but that trait can sometimes devolve into cynicism. Luckily, not all newspaper folks catch that bug. My favorite quote in Abernathy's book comes from Catherine Nelson, general manager of the *Rutland Herald*, who has worked in the industry for more than thirty years. When people tell her the field is dying, her response was:

"For too long, our industry was too slow and too boring. All that has changed. It's a challenging time, but it's also a very creative time, and that makes it an exciting and interesting time for people who are open to new ideas, believe in the value of newspapers, and want to help the industry solve problems and evolve."

Mark Palmer, a publisher from Tennessee who has worked in journalism since college and was working for his fifth newspaper when *Saving Community Journalism* was published, echoed Nelson's thoughts:

"We certainly live in interesting times. But I'm having fun in a different way than I was before. For those who are curious, it's a great time to be in the business."

More recently, student journalists at the University of Georgia now run *The Oglethorpe Echo* as a nonprofit, in what Barbara Allen said was "an interesting and promising development." Allen's 2021 write-up in Poynter, "How one university is taking over a small-town newspaper," explains how Dink NeSmith did not want to see the storied history of *The Oglethorpe Echo* newspaper fade into oblivion.

"In this model," NeSmith said in the piece, "maybe we might inspire some students to consider community journalism as a launching pad for their future career."

A more prominent paper, *The Wall Street Journal*, is now in the business of making product recommendations to people. In a small write-up in the paper in 2021 titled "Journal to Launch Commerce Venture," Alexandra Bruell wrote, "Commerce can provide a new revenue stream for publishers looking to diversify away from the uncertain advertising market." *WSJ* is not the only big-named paper to move into the commerce industry. BuzzFeed Inc. sells items online at BuzzFeed Shopping, while the New York Times Co. owns the website Wirecutter, which has product reviews and discounted items for sale. The mixing of commerce and journalism are realms of the newspaper business I don't recall discussing much in graduate school.

I respect how Jeff Jarvis cares about journalism, but I found his anything-goes, ultra-pro-digital outlook in *Geeks Bearing Gifts* to be off-putting at times. I didn't agree with his views on legacy media, which he dismisses as irrelevant. Worse, his practices and advice have possibly spawned a generation of social media-minded "journalists" who skim past the basics of what constitutes quality journalism. Jarvis's journalistic goals of enabling, organizing, and advocating for the betterment of the public are worthy but would be better dispersed in an objective-free, professional manner.

As it is, media choices these days can feel splintered and overwhelming. The Google-obsessed Jarvis is sometimes hard to take seriously when he claims public services such as answering questions, getting entertainment recommendations, connecting with friends, finding sales bargains, and sharing and discussing topics all qualify as news. These services may assist and engage the public, but the idea to transition journalists into the service realm does not, in my view, bode well for the legitimacy of the industry.

To be fair, one could likely find instances in which Jarvis's recommended digital enhancements for journalism organizations are already operating on numerous platforms that the public is utilizing—and those practical and well-placed services have likely only increased as technology has advanced. Though it's necessary to adapt with the digital times, news organizations cannot and should not be everything to everybody; they must stick with what is genuine news and do *that* well, especially if they want to earn the public's trust.

Journalism students should be exposed to both practical and pioneering teachings, and to his credit, Jarvis is a huge proponent of data mining, correctly calling it an "attitude" that journalists should acquire. His strong support of FOIA rights and his efforts toward getting the government to increase the dissemination of data and make it digitally accessible for everybody are admirable.

When done responsibly, content curation shows promise as being a valuable method of creating robust articles. The sixty-two-page piece "Newsroom Curators & Independent Storytellers: Content Curation as a New Form of Journalism," written by Federico Guerrini, provides valuable information on why curation matters and how to collect and verify user-generated content. He relates one instance in which U.S. journalists were barred from reporting in New York but still able to attain significant information, and how mainstream media outlets were able to generate digitally savvy content for large-scale world events.

Guerrini explains in his piece how "curation now plays an important role in how news stories are created by newsrooms (or freelancers) and then delivered to an audience."

"A new professional figure is increasingly gaining importance," Guerrini writes in the introduction. "The content curator, a word used to define a person who selects the best information found online with regard to its quality and relevance, aggregates it, linking to the original source of news, and provides context and analysis."

Jarvis, amid his railing against the news establishment and throwing out a laundry list of digital solutions from both well-known and obscure platforms, also recognizes the benefits of curation in today's journalism. He sees great value in hyperlinking within articles, discovering the best content to share with others, and complementing personal work with the help of the would-be journalists of the world.

"These are all skills needed in news today in a new and messy ecosystem of many voices, some good and some reliable, many not," he writes.

The "many not" aspect of this viewpoint is where one could picture Kovach and Rosenstiel recommending caution when curating content. Even Jarvis is wary of it.

As described in chapter two of this book, another useful and burgeoning tool for reporters is the availability of data to enhance an article's narrative. The report *The Art and Science of Data-Driven Journalism*, written by Alexander Benjamin Howard, says the practice of accumulating data is not new. These days, however, journalists can gather information extensively online via cloud computing and open-source software. The data acquired by journalists, in fact, is only limited by how hard they are willing to work to find it, and facts and records are not that difficult to discover nowadays, especially after journalists receive proper training.

"The open question in 2014 is not whether data, computers, and algorithms can be used by journalists in the public interest, but rather, how, when, where, why, and by whom," Howard writes. "Today, journalists can treat all of that data as a source, interrogating it for answers as they would a human."

Still, data sources are not factually foolproof. A great deal of information out there is formulated by homo sapiens, and humans are fallible. "Embrace skepticism" when seeking data, advises Howard, who wrote in his article that better tools created in the future will further assist data-driven journalists.

Deep into Jeff Sonderman's aforementioned article, "Unlocking mobile revenue and audience," is an embedded video featuring a talk by *The Elements of Journalism* co-author Tom Rosenstiel, who was the former executive director of the American Press Institute. The presentation is titled "What role do professional journalists play when anyone can publish?" and Rosenstiel begins it by relating the outlooks of professionals in the field who either subscribe to a notion of journalists' greatly diminished importance or those who believe the industry should not change one bit.

"This argument that we need journalists or we don't need journalists misses the point," says Rosenstiel. "It's a false dichotomy."

As noted earlier, Rosenstiel and Kovach don't discount digital technology in journalism—in today's news world, such thinking is elemental. But Rosenstiel complements this point in the video presentation by relating several advantageous components trained journalists bring to the news world: access to important people, storytelling and news-gathering skills, and the disciplines of an open mind and verification.

Expanding on these disciplines, Rosenstiel says journalists should approach a topic or person in a way that does not have an activist bent, is not propagandist, and is not politically motivated. She shouldn't judge and write until all viewpoints are explored. This approach requires humility, according to Rosenstiel, a concept Professor Rich Martin taught.

In a section titled "Listen to Mom" in the book *Living Journalism* by Martin, he relates how journalist Emily Siner wasn't sure how to interview individuals whose outlooks on current events might stir up controversy and inflame readers. So she contacted—who else?—her mom to see how she might handle such interviews. Her non-journalist mother recommended not approaching the interviews in a controversial way—approach them, she said, in a learning frame of mind.

"That advice changed the demeanor of Siner's questions," Martin wrote in his book. "It's human nature to jump to judgments and, as a journalist, thinking about ulterior motives is part of the job. But you can get to the real story if you start from a place of natural curiosity."

In the chapter "Independence from Faction" in *The Elements of Journalism*, the authors write about how certain well-known journalists shirk accountability in front of the public they are supposed to inform impartially and without influence. Television personality and longtime political writer and commentator George Will, for instance, wrote a column in 2003 about the leadup of the U.S. invasion in Iraq that may have been shaped by the viewpoint of an individual whose advisory board he sat on. Will made $25,000 for every board meeting he attended, yet he said his "business is my business" when pressed by peers about the conflict of interest.

As noted in the same book, Will was equally testy when confronted by reporters about giving a glowing summation of a Ronald Reagan speech in 1980 that he helped the future president craft.

"Journalism is now infested with persons who are 'little moral thermometers' dashing about taking temperatures, spreading, as confused moralists will, a silly scrupulosity and other confusions," Will said.

I respect George Will—and his fancily worded diatribe has merit, perhaps more than ever these days—but it was disappointing to read about some of his questionable behavior as a journalist. As Rosenstiel and Kovach point out, Will was essentially dismissing the legitimacy of the ethics of journalism, not a good thing if you care about the profession, which I'm sure he does.

This is not to say that journalists aren't allowed to have personal feelings or a point of view when they write, according to Rosenstiel and Kovach, who briefly profile columnist William Safire, of *The New York Times*, at the start of chapter five. According to the authors, Safire, who started his career as a speechwriter for Richard Nixon, was "a dyed-in-the-wool conservative who could skewer adversaries and end careers, and be strident when moved to be." Yet the deceased Safire garnered plenty of acclaim and was revered when he retired after more than thirty years in the business. Safire said that to get to the truth, journalists must sift through multiple realms of loyalties that can tie together. Rosenstiel and Kovach note that the Pulitzer Prize-winning journalist's diligence in pursuing the truth helped him identify when those on the inside were avoiding an issue or spinning an account.

"He was his own man, still conservative, but now working for his readers," Rosenstiel and Kovach write.

The authors believe that Safire's brand of journalism offered truth, a watchdog mentality, and a starting point for reasoned debate. They also say that opinion-shaped journalism is indispensable, even in an age when everyone can publish anything, and organizations can slant the news in their favor. Rosenstiel and Kovach list Thomas Friedman, Paul Gigot, Nick Lemann, Robert Caro, David Brooks, Paul Krugman, and David Halberstam as dedicated journalists who have deeply examined past high-profile issues, writers who would "be castigated rather than honored" if journalism were revered for its inauthenticity.

Amanda Hess of *Slate* displays a good columnist's sense of scrutiny in the article "Feminism Can Stand Without Jackie," a piece about feminists who gave their support for "Jackie," the featured subject in the bungled *Rolling Stone* article titled "A Rape on Campus: A Brutal Assault and Struggle for Justice at UVA," written by Sabrina Rubin Erdely. This allegiance to the apparent victim, and all rape victims in general, occurred even after numerous holes surfaced in Erdely's article. Bizarrely, the mistakes and oversights in the piece only propelled the feminists' mission without pause.

Hess was persistent and thorough in unravelling the *Rolling Stone* article. She implements humor to keep her piece entertaining ("*Rolling Stone's* editors have pledged to reinvestigate the tale themselves, and after the magazine's disastrous first round, I suspect that their project will be about as useful as O.J. Simpson's search for the real killers."), and she identifies those on the margins who cry foul over any rape story that has inaccuracies, saying these people are both "not reasonable" and in short supply.

Like Safire in his heyday, Hess wants to reveal the truth, which is why she argues for a true reinvestigation of Erdely's article. She asks: shouldn't students at the University of Virginia rightfully know if a group of gang rapists is roaming the campus? Was the university's initial response to the allegations appropriate? And should Jackie's friends be called upon to tell their side of the story?

"Carefully examining the *Rolling Stone* debacle and taking rape seriously as a national problem are not incompatible goals; we are capable of walking and chewing gum at the same time," Hess writes.

All journalists can likely agree that one of the most important aspects of journalism is the supporting effect it can have on communities, from informing citizens to stimulating the economy. Social media platforms have provided a fresh, effective way for newspapers to engage community members, according to the book *Saving Community Journalism* by Penelope Muse Abernathy, who relates the practices of Sallie See, editor of the *Hampshire Review* in West

Virginia. Abernathy writes that See is constantly on the newspaper's Facebook page reaching out to readers, doing everything from cheering on local sports teams to spotting posted pictures to use in her paper. These are tactics Jeff Jarvis would likely approve of.

Regarding her Facebook exploits on behalf of the newspaper, See says in the book, "It's the best way to stay on top of everything going on in this community."

Creative enterprises are happening within journalism in the academic realm, as well. In the *American Journalism Review* article titled "Journalism Schools Add Courses in Sports, Emerging Technology," Emily Wordsman describes inventive college-level courses such as Super Bowl Reporting and Glass Journalism, along with fresh degrees in the fields of social journalism and sports journalism, coursework that was developed to cater to students' interests and the new types of jobs in journalism becoming available.

Journalists may be at their most useful to the public when in the watchdog role, notifying citizens when businesses, government officials, and institutions abuse power, to the detriment of society. When done independently and without public pandering and corporate influence, investigative journalism, an "independent monitor of power," as Rosenstiel and Kovach write in chapter six, gives the profession a good name and a feel of high-quality communication. Top-notch investigative journalism allows public-health issues to come to light, puts a spotlight on underserved individuals in society, and sometimes leads to taxpayers not getting fleeced.

"It was the watchdog role that made journalism, to use James Madison's phrase, 'a bulwark of liberty,'" the authors write.

According to Rosenstiel and Kovach, the writings of early investigative journalists of the nineteenth century enthralled a public that was mostly ignorant of abuses by those in power, "creating an immediate and enthusiastic popular following." Such writing is still popular today and deemed crucial by the public and politicians within both major government parties, according to the authors. Investigative journalism, while expensive for news organizations, is needed as much as ever, but not the shoddy, sensationalized work that sometimes takes place. The topics covered in authentic watchdog journalism can lead to changing society for the better.

Investigative journalists from *The Wall Street Journal,* for example, uncovered in 2021 a slew of federal judges who were breaking the law by presiding over cases that involved companies they owned stock in. Some of these judges claimed to be surprised and were apologetic in the article. A piece in WSJ not long after, "Bill Would Toughen Stock-Trading Rules for Federal Judges," followed-up on the issue, stating at one point, "The Senate version of the stock-trading reporting bill, called the Courthouse Ethics and Transparency Act, would require judges to comply with the same law that applies to the president, vice president, presidential-appointed administration officials, senators and House members, according to congressional aides and a draft of the bill."

Newspapers are filled with depressing news every day. But when journalists work toward keeping those in power in check, society also wins, and justice is often served in readers' eyes.

Professor Ehrlich gave us a choice of intriguing books to read and analyze that covered varied realms of journalism and culture. I chose to read *Culture Crash: The Killing of the Creative Class* and had some fun in the intro of my essay. I titled the piece "Saving the World from Mediocrity," and it began like this:

YouTube has the platform to take us back in time, so let's reverse our lives nearly 27 years and revisit 1988. We're standing on an airport tarmac in Salt Lake City on an October day that is gorgeously sunny.

Low brown mountains fill parts of the landscape as the private airplane named "Hystouria #1" warms up for a flight to Portland, Oregon. At times during the amateurishly shot video its propellers spin madly and the engine screams at a fevered pitch.

As the young and famous rock band waits patiently to head on board, likely anxious to wrap up a tour that has lasted forever, the videographer, Ian Jeffery, questions a large man who wears dark shades and sports a prominent drooping mustache. He's an imposing figure with thick, jet-black hair and a tough-guy Brooklyn accent.

Jeffery: Having been the founding member of the production club here, how do you feel about this year?

Founding-member Tough Guy: "Well, let me put it to you this way. This is the best one I've ever heard about, none less done. Now, those guys over there (points to the members of Def Leppard) ... bunch o' beautiful humans. I wanted to thank them from the bottom of my swimming pool back home that I've put in since this little tour began eighteen fucking months ago."

At this point the tough guy has taken off his sunglasses and is staring intently into the camera. His round face features a prominent double chin. He's wearing a turquoise polo shirt and a faded jean jacket, both of which encompass the camera's entire frame.

"Beautiful thing as it is," he continues. "Oh, also, did I mention the Mustang, and the house payment?"

He laughs. You can tell he's showing off, bragging about all the money he's made. The guy really does feel lucky.

"Thank you so much, boys. Appreciate it."

Author Scott Timberg doesn't care about rock stars like Def Leppard in his book Culture Crash: The Killing of the Creative Class. He might, however, find the aforementioned interview interesting. After all, Founding-member Tough Guy made good money assisting lavish rock stars. He was part of a team that helped musicians succeed, highlighting the fact that artists of all types need this support system. Heavy metal rockers like Def Leppard crisscrossed the nation on gigantic, hugely profitable tours back then, but the world is a different place now—for musicians, for animators, for painters, for writers, for architects, for graphic designers, for sculptors, and for roadies like Tough Guy, who made a nice living that many of today's artists and their entourages can only dream of.

Timberg says today's music industry has been eviscerated by streaming music services and illegal piracy, but his argument as to why the creative class has been gutted, on all levels, goes beyond technology, which is part of what makes Culture Crash such an eye-opening read. Timberg, who has spent twenty years writing about a broad array of artists—from piano tuners to underground cartoonists to successful authors—would perhaps stand up for the brash guy in the "Backstage Hysteria 17 Def Leppard" video on YouTube. Individuals like the Tough Guy, after all, play a big role in helping others promote their artistry.

"While the fading fortunes of the creators of culture is alarming," says Timberg, "it's equally disturbing that their often-mocked supporting casts—record store clerks, roadies, critics, publicists, and supposedly exploitative record label folks—are being forced out of the culture industry."

I liked this book for numerous reasons. Right away, I recognized Timberg as a kindred spirit who enjoys writing about art and talking to artists in diverse realms. He has had great success in this line of work, and his financial troubles that open the book will make readers angry, and possibly a bit worried. Timberg's stated numbers are sobering: eighty percent of reporters and critics covering the arts for print publications have been laid off since 2000, according to ArtsJournal.com. When he uses the phrase "cheapening of the culture" early on, you can't help but think of a slew of reviews on Amazon reviewed by people getting their books via Kindle Unlimited or listening to unlimited music on Spotify or paying for movie-streaming services such as Netflix.

A former bookseller and music manager at Barnes & Noble in the 1990s, I can relate to the retail clerks that Timberg writes about and supports, often independently minded folks who can intelligently discuss music, movies, and books with customers who want thoughtful advice prior to making purchases. These retailers are also part of the creative class, according to the author, and with video stores, record stores, and bookstores having closed by the thousands in the U.S., their talents are not being utilized, their interests are perhaps going unfulfilled, and their camaraderie with like-minded people has sadly vanished. Timberg believes *a part of people's communities has been lost because of the changed retail environment in which clerks have disappeared.*

"They've been, over the decades, important conduits between consumers and culture—and their workplaces a training ground and meeting spot for some of our best writers, filmmakers, and bands," Timberg writes.

The class settled into a routine, like they do. One thing Issues in Journalism showed me was that creative ideas abounded when it came to thinking about new business models for journalism. Students today who enter the field of journalism often do so because they feel called to it, no different from students twenty years ago or forty years ago. But this noble calling has its share of uncertainties these days, which includes being able to make a decent living wage as a journalist.

Forward-thinking Jeff Jarvis has no shortage of ideas on how to create business models that could possibly boost the field he cares about. His list of answers is dizzying to read at times, but his passion is admirable. Jarvis has hope.

"It's not easy," he admits at the end of his book *Geek Bearing Gifts*. "But there is no better time to teach journalism and no better time to become a journalist."

Working for legacy media outlets is still a bright possibility. Encompassing well-known news outlets such as ABC, CNN, and *The New York Times*, legacy media also extends locally to news organizations in cities across America such as in Champaign, Illinois, where outlets such as WICD and *The News-Gazette* exist. Starting out by interning or working in legacy media can provide new journalists with useful experiences; such reporters, in fact, may opt to stay in well-established environments if they can.

Advantages to beginning a journalism career at, say, a small newspaper such as the *Mahomet Citizen*, like I did, include having an established audience to read your work online or in print; receiving a paycheck that may not be large but is steady; getting the opportunity to do original reporting, a task that is becoming less prominent in an age of aggregation; and working among professionals who know the area and can provide invaluable reporting and advertising advice.

Kovach and Rosenstiel offer suggestions to keep journalism relevant in chapter eight of *The Elements of Journalism*, at times even calling to mind the more avant-garde prospects that Jarvis suggests.

"Forms such as the inverted pyramid for news stories were so formulaic that, although the stories modeled on them were filled with facts and detail, they failed to engage readers," they write.

The authors focus on audience engagement in this chapter, offering advice on how to concentrate on readers and the story, as well as how to embrace technology in journalism and use it sensibly. They cite journalism teacher Jay Rosen in one section as someone who knows "how to orient news more toward the interests of citizens rather than needs of the journalists' traditional formats." At the start of chapter eight, they talk about journalist Lara Setrakian, who used her experiences as a foreign correspondent at ABC and Bloomberg Television to begin a cutting-edge website called Syria Deeply.

"The good news is that the same technology that devastated the economic foundation of commercial news in the beginning of the new century has also unleashed a profound new wave of creativity," they write.

In other realms, data-driven upstarts such as *The Upshot, FiveThirtyEight,* and *Vox* are examples of how the splintering of media is watering down salaries and making people's heads spin with so much online information. James Ball describes the challenges these publications face in his article, "The Upshot, Vox and FiveThirtyEight: data journalism's golden age, or TMI?" In the piece, he questions what format data-driven articles should take, and what it is that readers want to see. Are these ever-growing types of publications news-breakers or analyzers? Is there a proven model they should follow, or do they carve out a new way to convey data? And the most stimulating question in the article: "How much is too much?"

"Are we being over-served, under-served, or have we now hit the Goldilocks point?" he asks.

No matter a journalist's desire (or not) for reams of available data that can potentially be a source for news stories, data-driven articles are here to stay and have made a big difference in modern-day journalism stories. Unfortunately, many news organizations, such as the ones mentioned in Ball's article, have a fleeting existence. This fly-by-night state of various news platforms makes it hard to keep track and make sense of what trends are real and what outlets are the most trustworthy.

Beacon, for instance, was a site in which journalists contributed content and readers could choose the journalists they wanted to subscribe to for $5 a month, with access to the other writers. This enterprise is described in the article "Beyond the paywall: Beacon wants to make it easier for journalists to become like Andrew Sullivan," written by Mathew Ingram.

"Beacon isn't trying to replace existing outlets ... it's just trying to supplement that existence with something more regular, and something that involves writers connecting directly with their loyal fans," Ingram writes.

But I wondered: how much loyalty can readers feel toward unknown writers on a site like Beacon? How much supplemental material do readers need? Why would an aspiring journalist, or even an established one, want to put his energies into work that likely won't get widely read or make a difference in society? Can such a publication afford to do in-depth investigative pieces, which at the time was diminishing in journalism?

It turns out these questions were valid. When I recently clicked on a hyperlink to Beacon's website via the aforementioned article by Ingram, I came to a nearly blank page that read, "This site can't be reached."

In the piece "The Wolf at the door: Should journalism worry about content marketing?" Michael Meyer describes glossy pet publications dedicated to making money and providing extraordinary customer service. "Brand newsrooms," he writes, are everywhere, forgoing the help of traditional media and furthering the decline of ad revenue.

Meyer brings up worthwhile points about why this sort of advertising has potentially negative consequences for the future of journalism. He describes top-notch marketing copy as writing that combines news factoids with customer engagement and promotion. When this trio of elements is put together skillfully, he writes, it's not discernible from a journalistic newspaper article. He goes on to say that journalists and the public should worry even more when restaurants like Chipotle tackle serious issues in their copywriting.

"Brands are really good at finding new ways to adopt the aspects of journalism that most appeal to the public—and they're getting better at it every day," he writes.

Companies want to sell their products, and native advertising helps them do that. It also provides writing jobs and good money to sustain the very journalists who sometimes view it unfavorably. This growing and evolving form of advertising feels uncomfortable, but it hasn't dissolved journalism just yet.

We covered this topic with Brant Houston in the Reporting II course I took in 2013. He says advertorials should be clearly labeled as such at the top of the piece and have different font than the regular content to clearly distinguish it. He also believes publications should carefully examine what their standards are for accepting advertorials.

"And I would say I'm even stronger on this now because with all the good things happening in nonprofit newsrooms with lots of integrity, there are some nonprofit newsrooms with dark money. There are some newsrooms that appear to be nonprofit that are not only dark money [but are] totally partisan and try and make money off what I would say—it sounds so weird to say—real fake news. I mean, they're just making stuff up."

A local rag called *Prime Life Times* periodically runs an ad titled "Seven years without a cold?" The subhead reads, "Copper in new device stops cold and flu." Houston's practical advice about clearly labeling advertorials is noticeably ignored here, with the wording "(paid advertisement)" showing up in italics and small font at the bottom of the questionable piece.

Another interesting—and perhaps less threatening—business model to help sustain news organizations is relayed in an article by Kevin Loker, "The best strategies for generating revenue through events." News organizations holding events may seem like an unnatural revenue generator, but Loker convincingly argues that substantial profits can be gained and trust established.

"Events are a proven way to diversify revenue that, if done right, are significantly harder to disrupt than other revenue models," he writes. "They deepen connections with audiences and sponsors. They reinforce multiple values of a publishing brand. And they can grow."

But Loker also relates the conflicts of interest that can arise between business and editorial interests when news outlets hold events. His advice is to be as transparent as possible and to "structure for separation." Much like native advertising, readers must be alert and perceptive. April Hinkle, former director of business development at *The Texas Tribune*, didn't sound worried about the separation of church and state issue, so to speak: "Our audience is very well educated. They're going to smell a rat."

The measure of good journalism is often gauged by its truthfulness and ability to help sustain a self-governing society. Given those attributes of the past, the article "Who cares if it's true? Modern-day newsrooms reconsider their values," written by Marc Fisher, is both discouraging and heartening. On the one hand, Fisher talks about the brashness of *BuzzFeed* journalists and their disdain toward the "old newspaper way of doing things." Online quizzes, pointless viral videos, seamy click-bait headlines—it's enough to make old-time news junkies seriously worried about the future. Then again, to its credit, *BuzzFeed* has bolstered its news department in the past and has made admirable headway toward covering important topics. The organization has hired more copy editors, and its writers have won noteworthy journalism awards. Like much of today's journalism, *BuzzFeed* is producing serious fare that runs parallel with the frivolous.

Fisher conveys the budding nuances happening at *BuzzFeed* between hardened journalists and newcomers on the scene. "What if conciliation is at hand?" he writes, pointing out the importance of releasing news items speedily (such as through tweeting), while noting that the younger generation is gravitating more toward accuracy in a hyper-connected news age.

"It's about finding the right middle point," he says. "Some degree of perfectionism turns out to be good for business, and absolute perfectionism can prevent great journalism from ever happening at all."

This positive cross-generational collaboration bodes well. One wonders how much more successful it could be if citizens were educated in news literacy starting at a young age, no different than taking required classes on U.S. government. This issue is brought to light in

Lindsay Bernstein's piece, "Can news literacy grow up?" which advocates for such curriculum. Commenting on the proliferation of sponsored content, "glossy magazines," and "slick docu-ads that look and sound a lot like journalism," Bernstein says the need for news literacy is required more than ever, though she admits that research has shown the effects of news literacy education diminish after a year.

Along those lines, Jeff Jarvis offers his best writing and most coherent direction in the "Afterword" section of *Geeks Bearing Gifts*. The journalism training that he and others are doing at the CUNY Graduate School of Journalism is intriguing, even trailblazing. It's possible that Jarvis has proudly witnessed one or more of his entrepreneurial-focused students implementing new, bona fide business models that have bolstered journalism.

The thoughts of Bernstein and Jarvis reinforce how education in general underpins future interests and skills. Why do certain populations elsewhere in the world care more about important news than Americans? Perhaps it's because they are better educated.

The questions may be as valid now as they were when I was in graduate school: what can help save journalism, and how can aspiring journalists land jobs that pay well and provide stable careers?

Sometimes it feels right to talk about the basics, things like creating content that will entice readers and keep them coming back. Jay Rosen is a no-nonsense, forward-thinking media executive who runs the blog PressThink. In one of his posts, he discusses what he learned from a person in media who wanted to develop a "full stack" way of relating news. Full stack is a software term and philosophy that Rosen wanted to apply to his field.

He was inspired by this layered approach of conveying news, which begins with thinking about what is newsworthy and then designing an accompanying look. The idea is not to regurgitate what has been done, but to instead create original content and then go beyond only one aspect of the story. Rosen calls such reporting "thought layers." Every outlet can report the same news, he mentions at the end of the post, but going full stack on competitors requires the ambition to make stories specialized.

"That means defining the beat the way no one else defines it, and coming up with a mission that differs from the industry standard," he writes.

In an era of aggregated reporting that can sound the same, Rosen's thoughts on specialized journalism have merit and could be one way to help sustain the field.

A burgeoning type of writing that feels like the opposite of the full-stack-approach is having robots do the work for writers. This would allow news outlets to release breaking stories at lightning speed—feed the machine the correct data and hit "Enter" on the keyboard—while fact-checking, presumably, would still be done by humans.

The bleak thought regarding writing by robots is that it could put many writers out of work and destroy yet another part of an industry in this digitized age. This is a possibility as writing by machines becomes more prominent. According to a Shelley Podolny article written in 2015, "If an Algorithm Wrote This, How Would You Even Know?" most news will be created by computers by the mid-2020s. Robots are even writing books these days, according to the piece.

"We're on a slippery slope," Podolny writes.

Brant Houston, however, has a different outlook on robot writing, saying that algorithms have the well-developed capacity these days to write certain kinds of stories—a good thing, he believes, given that the number of newspaper reporters has dwindled drastically. Houston envisions a "digital system" that would allow subscribers to pick and choose the news alerts on crime or zoning that they want to read about, perhaps in areas where they live.

"Anybody who wrote a lot of these stories knows," he said. "We always joked a machine could write this story. Well, it turns out it can. It just needs a human being to read through it before it's sent out to make sure it makes sense."

Robots or not, journalism desperately needs an injection of money and civically minded people who care enough to help sustain it. In the piece "The Death and Life of Great American Newspapers" by John Nichols and Robert W. McChesney, Walter Isaacson said:

"It is now possible to contemplate a time in the near future when major towns will no longer have a newspaper and when magazines and network news operations will employ no more than a handful of reporters."

This projection has come true and continues, but there is always hope.

Professor Ehrlich said that in his gloomier moments, he is glad he's no longer teaching journalism on a regular basis. In this frame of mind, he wonders if it's even possible nowadays for journalism organizations to attract more than just niche audiences. He hopes there are "news products" out there that can appeal to more than just one side of the political spectrum, but he has his doubts.

If Ehrlich were teaching Issues in Journalism now, he said he would pose fundamental questions to the class revolving around broad-based journalism audiences. He wonders if journalistic organizations can afford to write off folks who don't believe in truth-based *anything*, let alone truth-based, evidence-based journalism. He observes social media and people's wide-ranging responses to COVID-19, for example. Ehrlich's current research has set his mind a little more at ease, but he is still concerned.

"In doing historical research as I've been doing the last year or two, actually longer than that, I do realize now that this isn't totally new, that this has always been an issue," he said. "But it does certainly feel extremely acute now, and the implications of that for journalism, let alone democracy, are concerning."

Ehrlich also has his optimistic moments regarding journalism, and there are reasons for hope on multiple fronts, he believes. Though far from a firebrand, Ehrlich sounded more defiant than I remember him as he related a cliché that journalism professors often convey, as well as how things could be going forward.

"For several years now, journalism educators have been telling students, 'This is the most exciting time to be studying journalism and entering the profession because you can help reinvent it,'" Ehrlich said. "And I sometimes think that students must roll their eyes when they hear that. But I do think that there's a substantial amount of truth to that. That it does give you more freedom to take chances to say, you know, screw it, this is our political stance. This is where we're coming from. We're going to be totally transparent about it. We are going to be committed to truth-based, evidence-based reporting. And if that's something that you do not accept as an acceptable version of your truth, then so be it. That's fine. Go forth and find your own media. We're not going to try to reach you. We're not going to try to win your trust because that's a losing proposition. We're going to focus our attention and energy on doing what we think is important, and we're going to find the audience willing to support that."

Ehrlich then said he believes people *do* want to support truth-based, evidenced-based journalism, which he said is redundant because journalism is, by itself, supposed to be based in truth. He used the example of Wikipedia as being a source of information that promotes a neutral point of view, in the sense that the crowd-sourced, crowd-funded online platform relies on writers who embrace neutrality and keep the agitators in check when something controversial is written. He called these fact-checking individuals "citizen editors" and "citizen journalists."

"So, there are models of neutrality," Ehrlich said. "So that, I think, is cause for optimism that more traditional models—going back to Kovach and Rosenstiel and what we were reading from them—might embrace."

Before we hung up, Ehrlich said that journalism will keep going somehow, someway. I heard optimism in his voice. "Certainly, these kinds of questions we're wrestling with now are longstanding issues that have no easy resolution, but they're important to keep thinking about."

Chapter 5: More Than a Big Book Club and an Intro to Literary Journalism

The first time I ever spoke with Professor Walt Harrington *may* have been in the spring of 2015, when he called me at work to tell me a story I'd written had won third place in the College of Media's Marian and Barney Brody Creative Feature Article Writing Award in Journalism—the story about Louis Postlewaite Jr. I was thrilled about the news, but I also remember thinking how remarkable it was that *the* Walt Harrington had called me to relate it.

I didn't know tons about Harrington at the time, but I wasn't oblivious to the fact that he had a sterling reputation as a revered storyteller in journalism. During my time in graduate school, I received group emails from him, in which he invited Media students to sign up for one of his evening classes. He made the course sound like one big cozy conversation about journalism books. I kept the invitation in the back of my mind as graduation day loomed closer. It was intriguing.

Then again, I may have first talked to Harrington on another occasion, an afternoon in which I had used my lunch hour on campus to head over to Gregory Hall to watch a presentation on a journalism topic, I think by a visiting alumna of the college. Though it was undoubtedly a stimulating talk, I remember zilch about it. What I *do* recall, however, is Harrington in the audience, several seats to my right, asking me out of the blue, prior to the event, if I was a certain person. He had me mistaken for someone else, but to this day I wonder if he was simply trying to make conversation. I told him I wasn't the guy he thought I was, and I think I introduced myself, but that was the extent of our exchange. We both stared ahead in our seats after that, silently waiting for the talk to begin. In retrospect, I wish I had talked to him more that day.

Our paths would cross again, however, and Harrington's influence would completely change my course of study in journalism and have a far-reaching effect long after I walked through the halls of Gregory.

I'd reached a point in my master's program where I finally had a bit of a break, in the sense that I could now take a three-credit elective course. Elective classes, at least to me, have an off-the-beaten-path sort of feel. Their descriptions sounded less intense, even fun, though perhaps that's overstating things. In the end, I chose to enroll in Great Books of Journalism, the night class Professor Harrington had encouraged students to sign up for via email. The course sounded appealing to an avid reader like me, and Harrington's passion toward the class was also a deciding factor. The class sounded like what people do in a book club, with required writing tasks interspersed throughout.

But Great Books of Journalism was more than just a large book club, as I came to find out. As we read the assigned books, we were often asked by Harrington to contemplate *how* the writers were coming up with their material, and in a way in which we as readers trusted what they were producing. Here are some gems from my handwritten class notes:

- Journalists make choices at the start on how to report. Can create limitations.
- Authors bring personality to story. This kind of work honors that people bring a special story. This is the heart of literary journalism.
- Being there is an opportunity that's foolish to squander.
- Go where the material takes you in nonfiction writing.
- Learn how to write so that it feels like you're there, even if you're not there (Boo, Finkel).
- Tone of story should follow tone of subjects.
- All facts in journalism should be defensible.
- Recognize your biases; be thoughtful about them. Possible to get better at working around biases.
- As a journalist, pick point of view that has the most validity. Must be humble when reporting and reaching a conclusion. Journalists have a responsibility to decide and then connect their point of view.
- Complexity of human choice makes for great stories, an unfamiliar ride for readers.
- Conceptual ideas can be woven in (artful aspect). Don't have to hit people over the head.
- "Pulling a thread" gives work unity, makes it organic.
- Collection of facts is great, but what is the larger picture?
- Good journalists interweave commentary into description in expert fashion.
- Power of details and role they play in creating authenticity.
- Look at technical side of things. Intricacies of things can be very interesting. Ride on passion, knowledge of subject.
- Journalists can do more than just "let the camera role." (Background, descriptions, inside experiences, etc.)
- History is constantly being rethought. Historians present new info. Takes on things change over the decades. Journalists use tools that historians don't. Interview everyone.
- Good interviewers can make conversations seem natural, fluent.
- To evoke experience or a place, do something no one else is.
- Not doing deep enough reporting if you don't wrestle with decisions.

Beyond the books, Professor Harrington had numerous learning objectives in his class that ranged from the importance of thinking critically and independently to relating to students "the principles and laws of freedom of speech and press," as written in the course syllabus. He wanted us to know that journalism could go well beyond ho-hum articles with no heart. "The writers of these books are not simply conduits for passing along accurate information," Harrington wrote in the syllabus. "They are thinkers, observers and storytellers. They take responsibility for *making sense* of information, sometimes in ways that are deeply personal and idiosyncratic. And they do so by aiming to tell their stories in ways that make them fascinating to readers."

On the first evening of class, I walked into the classroom and saw a large circle of desks, all of them filled. From the outset, led by Walt Harrington's insights and questions, we talked about interesting and informative books, ones I likely never would have read if I hadn't taken the course. In my final sentence of the essay about the 1904 book *The History of the Standard Oil Company* by Ida M. Tarbell, I lamely wrote, "*Standard Oil* drilled the first hole for future tough-minded journalists wanting to expose the next unethical company."

Other books we read and talked about included the tomes *The Power Broker* by Robert A. Caro and *Let Us Now Praise Famous Men* by James Agee. We also read and discussed the much slimmer books *Oranges* by John McPhee and *Hiroshima* by John Hersey; and my two favorite reads, *The Good Soldier* by David Finkel and *Behind the Beautiful Forevers* by Katherine Boo (a book mentioned earlier from Brant Houston's class). My first paragraph on the essay I wrote about Finkel's book reveals an enthralled reader:

"I'll start with this cliché: The Good Soldier by David Finkel reads like a novel. Ralph Kauzlarich, the lieutenant colonel leading a courageous but eventually dispirited battalion of U.S. soldiers in Iraq, is the headstrong protagonist who is just nuanced enough to evoke admiration. Readers get an up-close look at his "It's all good" headspace and find out where that mentality comes from. Kauzlarich's wife, Stephanie, lent her emails to the author for the narrative, some of them intimate and loving. Later emails, phone calls, and letters from girlfriends, wives, and parents demonstrate mock complacency and extreme frustration over being separated from their loved ones for so long. Finkel grippingly captures the strained relationships."

One evening in class, I received back my essay on Agee's book from Harrington, who always graded them and wrote comments at the end of the paper. This particular remark said, "Nice, thoughtful job. Come in and talk sometime." Surprised to get such an invitation from one of the country's best-known literary journalism writers and teachers, I didn't wait long to email him and schedule a time to meet.

His office was large with a huge bookshelf. To this day, I regret not taking the time to look more carefully through all those books. Professor Harrington had just released his latest book, *Artful Journalism*, which he gave me, and I had brought him a copy of one of my independently published novels, *The Millionaire's Cross*, which I would extensively rewrite five years later. *Artful Journalism* is my favorite book ever written about the craft of writing.

He had two plush chairs that faced each other, so I eased into one of them and we talked for an hour. We chatted about the books we had written, our jobs, literary journalism, and I remember religion crept into the conversation. Harrington has a tough-minded aura and is whip smart, but he also has a kind, trustworthy way about him, which I think helps people feel comfortable in his presence. I'm sure these traits helped many an interviewee open up to him. Yet despite his approachable, welcoming personality, I rarely felt like I could match Harrington's stimulating thoughts or keep up with him when it came to our scholarly talks. The guy just has so much wisdom and eloquence about him.

When I left his office that afternoon, I wondered what, exactly, our meeting had been about. Was it nothing more than a friendly invitation or did the guy want something from me? A day or two later I discovered that he did indeed have an ulterior motive in getting to know me, but I didn't feel manipulated in the least. As it turned out, I would need something from Harrington as well.

One surprising occurrence in the Great Books of Journalism class was seeing my former boss's daughter, Jessica Elliott, in it. I'd first met her in 2007, when she was a preteen. For the most part, I hadn't been all that self-conscious about my more advanced age among the youngsters while in graduate school; but seeing this now-grown-up and intelligent young lady threw me for a loop and put the passage of time into the forefront.

Jessica was pursuing a bachelor's degree in theatre studies, with a concentration in directing and playwriting. She had begun her undergraduate career majoring in journalism and had briefly worked at *The Daily Illini.*

"The thing that drew me to journalism was the same thing that drew me to the theater," Jessica said. "It was telling stories. And it was connecting people. I like to tell people that I ended up doing the same thing, just with a different path."

Jessica earned her bachelor's degree in 2017 and went on to pursue a master's degree and certification to teach social studies in high school. To her, the principles of journalism taught in Harrington's class felt like a bridge toward what she would eventually convey to students. As a student teacher at Unity High School, not far from Champaign-Urbana, she taught the journalistic concepts of determining sources and evaluating bias and accuracy during history and civics lessons for juniors and seniors.

Her undergraduate years at Illinois impressed upon Jessica that "there is an art to science and there is a science to art." Though she thought her brain was hardwired toward artistry in her early college years, she discovered that implementing scientific knowledge and methods can also be a part of artistic endeavors. Taking Harrington's course helped her see the balance between science-based facts and creativity.

"I left that class knowing you could lend an artistry to [journalism] and you could still accurately and successfully report. Tell a story that is based in fact, but you could still put personality into it and give it humanity," she said.

Jessica appreciated how open Harrington was to hearing students' ideas and letting them talk about the readings in such a free-flowing, explorative way. At the same time, she noted his knowledge and experience in journalism and always looked forward to hearing his insights during classes.

Jessica said John Hersey's book was "very impactful" while Ida Tarbell's book was a "different type of writing that was exciting." But the book that left the biggest impression on her was James Agee's *Let Us Now Praise Famous Men.* She said Agee's vivid, intimate descriptions of the people he wrote about were undeniably absorbing. What she found fault with, however, and as was discussed in Harrington's class, were the photos in the book—no one was smiling in them. Anywhere. And Jessica and other students in the class found that hard to fathom.

"No one was smiling or having fun," she said of the photos taken by Walker Evans in Agee's book. "And it's very hard to believe that none of that was going on. So, it's that responsibility of showing the *full* scope of humanity and the full nature of that experience."

As a teacher, Jessica said it's her responsibility to capture the entire spectrum of the people and events she covers. Often, she said, not all historical events are fairly and fully documented. The winners of history, she believes, can be judicious in their documenting.

"And the narratives that they build and construct, and the things that they leave out, I see that more as a responsibility now because of my experience in [Harrington's] class," Jessica said.

On one page of my notes for this class, I wrote, "No one shows any joy in book. Same thing with the pictures. No mention of <u>love</u> for supposedly such a divine people. Professor think it's no accident. They created the tone."

That's not to say that Agee didn't do an outstanding job of accurately capturing the bleak lives of the families covered in his book. Many of the sad-looking photos in *Famous Men* could be authentic. Here's an excerpt of what I wrote in my class recap of the book:

Agee's observations about anything in his path, human or inanimate, are monumental, as if he's describing alien beings and objects unknown to all. When he writes about the sparseness within a sharecropper's house, the items have genuine meaning in a larger context. When he describes the pitiful education system in

Alabama, readers will lament over the circumstances and silently hope for massive change. When he scrutinizes poor people's clothes in the "Clothing" chapter, readers will find it fascinating or excruciatingly boring and a touch humiliating. Agee's anti-elitist writing includes long, meticulous passages; poetry and prayers; and even a question-and-answer session. Agee's journalistic skills shine beautifully when he spends the night at the Gudgers house. Rather than go straight to sleep, probably an impossible task anyway given the bed bugs, he absorbs everything and relates some of the most telling moments of the book. The physicality of what it's like to eat and sleep in such a house blasts into the consciousness, and suddenly readers know the true meaning of destitution.

Not long after our chat, Professor Harrington emailed me to say he needed assistance in updating his two WordPress websites. One was a bio site about Harrington and his work, and the other, intimatejournalism.com, was dedicated to the many literary journalism pieces by students that Harrington had edited over the years. He had discovered I was a communications professional cut out to do this sort of web work, and he was right. One of my proudest moments during graduate school, in fact, was helping him clean up and put in good order both of these websites, which needed some TLC. I was flattered he had asked me and even more surprised when he said he would set up a stipend from the university for my efforts. Along with the work on his websites, Harrington asked me to do some research for a project he was working on.

In this way, Walt Harrington and I got to know one another throughout the semester. We'd periodically meet in his office so I could give him updates on the website work, and as I continued on with the Great Books of Journalism course, I became more and more drawn to the craft of literary journalism.

My side-gig work on intimatejournalism.com that semester found its way into the first several paragraphs of the final essay I wrote for the Great Books of Journalism course, a piece straightforwardly titled "What I learned about journalism":

Many of my expanded ideas on how journalism can be taken to a new, inspirational level are contained in a great article on intimatejournalism.com called "A 4000-mile house call," written by Carey Sullivan. Working as a literary journalist in a poor Mayan village, Sullivan observed and took extensive notes she could utilize later, using the details to piece together sections that read like captivating scenes in a short story. She selected the best moments that worked for the article, leaving out what didn't work, and chose words that would help the prose flow smoothly.

Similar to a dedicated craftsman building a slaved-over chair, Sullivan constructed her article by immersing herself in her surroundings and building it with tried-and-true procedures, methods that writer John McPhee—a craftsman himself—would admire. She took pictures, for instance, and chatted intimately with the natives and her fellow U.S. volunteers to gain deeper insights.

Like writer William Least Heat Moon in the book Blue Highways, *Sullivan was the central character in her first-person story, an entertaining narrator who ultimately learned something about herself and the world during a journey she despised toward the end. Though different from traditional journalistic reporting and writing, Sullivan and Moon informed readers in detailed ways about life in varied locations, and they did so in an enjoyable, heartfelt manner that resonates.*

Prior to this class, I have read articles and long-form essays in the vein of Sullivan and Moon. Yet I've never learned the techniques used to create such compelling, humanistic pieces, and I perhaps overlooked the fact that such works capture provoking elements of society as effectively as traditional journalism, perhaps more so.

A little further down in the write-up, I wrote this:

As we learned in class, the authors of our readings are smart and tenacious journalists. In most cases they had extensive experience in the field, which led them to writing their landmark books. Outliers all of them, the authors are a conglomeration of data gatherers, expert interviewers, deep thinkers, craftspeople, unflagging researchers, poignant essayists, and brave immersion observers who set precedents within the broad sphere of what journalism can be.

As stated several times during the course, their methods can be studied and emulated to keep literary journalism alive. This work is doable, though the craft, according to Harrington in his book Artful Journalism, may best be practiced by those with an open mind and heart, and people who are willing to inquire broadly into personal details. "It's hard work," Harrington writes, "turning human emotions, feelings, and attitudes into facts." Amid the process, Harrington believes the industrious efforts to reach conclusions should be carried out humbly.

Katherine Boo, author of Behind the Beautiful Forevers, shares Harrington's passion for thought-provoking, in-depth journalism and feels the sought-after facts she strives for eventually rise up to make for more stimulating policy pieces in areas like poverty, which some may consider a humdrum subject. "I just believe that better arguments, maybe even better policies, get formulated when we know more about ordinary lives," Boo writes in the Author's Note section of her book.

Harrington notes in Artful Journalism that memorable work can only be accomplished by learning about and absorbing the "color" surrounding a person's life. This is done by conducting extensive interviews with the subject and her friends, family, acquaintances, enemies, and possibly beyond; researching the realms that matter most in the person's life; and imagining the individual you're writing about in a "grand fashion." The advice of Harrington, who studied the inexhaustible methods of Robert Caro, author of The Power Broker, is pertinent to all our class readings. Like James Agee, who wrote Let Us Now Praise Famous Men, Harrington aims for a certain spirit and human quality that is often missing in today's journalism, and he teaches the merits of doing work that is accurate and defensible.

Writers can learn from the systematic ways in which Harrington and Caro organize the info they gather so that the facts are easy to locate when it is time to write. Harrington recommends indexing all similar aspects of the story together, including references to people, events, and research, and then meticulously filing everything so that it is all easily searchable. For his part, Caro streamlined The Power Broker in a cutting-edge way by including a Note on Sources section, in which he listed the dates of all frequently interviewed subjects. He also included a bibliography and an extensive sources section that readers can use to verify how he got his information. The brilliance of these inclusions—methods that now may be taken for granted—is that the book was not slowed down by attribution or citations.

We learned that experienced literary journalists can produce memorable scenes even if they are not present during the moments they write about, a talent worth noting for aspiring writers. For example, author John Hersey went to Hiroshima nine months after the atomic bomb dropped on the city to write Hiroshima, which was credited as the first nonfiction book to read like a novel. The narratives are based solely on survivors' recollections, so Hersey had to know how he wanted to present his story, select the best profiles, and then ask questions that would extract the most in-the-moment happenings and multisensory details to make his characters and story come alive. Writers sometimes must deal with the circumstances and deadlines they have, and Hersey's circumstance in this case was visiting Japan well after the atomic bomb dropped.

Other examples include David Finkel using army reports, follow-up interviews, and other sources to create vivid scenes he didn't witness in Iraq. Additionally, Boo, who was present for most of the events in Beautiful Forevers, occasionally reconstructed events quickly by using documents and conducting interviews for moments she didn't see firsthand.

As the semester wound down, it was getting time for me to select a final project I wanted to do for my Master's Project (JOUR 515). I had the option of writing a thesis or doing an extensive journalism project. The latter sounded more intriguing to me and is what I ended up doing, but I must admit, writing a thesis would have also been a rewarding experience.

Often when I met with Harrington, I would hem and haw about whether I was capable of doing a final project on literary journalism. In my heart, I wanted to do it and told him so. At one point in these conversations, Harrington told me I probably wasn't up to the task since I had never taken his Literary Feature Writing course (JOUR 481). That plainspoken advice decided things for me. I contacted Brant Houston via email to see if he would be my graduate advisor for my final project. My plan was to take a stab at an investigative journalism piece. Houston said yes, and that was that.

But then the plan changed. I don't recall where I was or what I was doing, but I said to myself that I wanted more than anything to study literary journalism and write creative nonfiction stories during the end of my graduate career. I simply had to try. Like so many other writers before me, Harrington had pulled me into his world. He was retiring at the end of the semester after a long and fruitful career in academia, and here I was asking the poor guy to hang on a bit longer, to coach me along so I could publish an engaging and perfect literary journalism piece. I needed his wisdom to make my studies in journalism feel complete.

When I informed Harrington that I wanted him to be my graduate advisor, I could see a look of amusement and a hint of resignation on his bearded face. I think he knew it was what I genuinely wanted, and in some karmic kind of way, I think he thought serving as a graduate advisor on his way out might be a poignant way to cap off his career.

For my final project, we agreed I would sit in during his Literary Feature Writing course and participate in all of the discussions on writing and the student article critiques. I would also read all of the assigned readings and write the required number of literary journalism stories, which for me was two.

I ended up writing four pieces, and my work carried over into the summer semester.

Chapter 6: 'Over-braining'

Entire books have been written about the methods of literary journalism, but in a nutshell, this type of piece, sometimes referred to as creative nonfiction and longform journalism, is written in a way that feels like fiction, often with elements found in any good fictional narrative: interesting characters, well-described settings, an overarching theme, an engaging plot, riveting dialogue, and conflict and resolution, with the hoped-for added benefit of the person being covered, and possibly the reader, learning something valuable in the end. To do these things, good literary journalists use all five senses when reporting.

In the Literary Featuring Writing syllabus, Walt Harrington prepared the class to think and write in a scene and theme frame of mind as we attempted to try to find the "extraordinary in the ordinary." Writers in this realm take copious notes, take pictures (oftentimes to refer to for setting purposes), and record interviews, all the while making sure not to forget about the basics of journalism such as striving for the truth at all costs and using attribution when necessary. Several books in the class were required reading, but Professor Harrington also recommended in the syllabus numerous nonfiction books such as *Essays of E.B. White*, *The Sweet Science*, *The Warmth of Other Suns*, and *Slouching Toward Bethlehem*, among many others. In previous classes, I had learned about the importance of collecting good data in journalism; now Harrington was conveying that data points do not have to determine everything in a story. Feelings and emotions in humans count for a lot too.

At the conclusion of this course, my final one in graduate school, Harrington asked his students to write an essay about what they had learned about creative nonfiction. Two sections of the paper I turned in for this assignment stand out to me:

Receiving feedback from discerning readers was an interesting experience. The process of hearing what my peers thought about two of my articles was interesting and ranged from the minute to the conceptual. Having numerous "editors" can be an intimidating way to work, but it is also valuable. At times, following the thoughts of fellow students regarding my pieces was hard to discern and a bit overwhelming. What surprised me about this free-flowing method of analyzation in class was how a variety of people saw my work in different ways, and how they made varied recommendations that I never would have thought of. Beyond my articles, I was impressed with the way students in class were so perceptive and noticed issues or had ideas for stories that did not cross my mind. Students produced solid revisions throughout the semester, and it was fun to see the work improve.

This assessment was cheerier and more hopeful sounding than how I actually felt by the time the class ended that spring semester. The below excerpt from the same paper is more honest:

I enjoy reading literary journalism pieces more than writing them. My favorite part of this class was reading and later discussing pieces in "Intimate Journalism" and "Next Wave." Most of the stories in these books were riveting, and the "Next Wave" articles particularly reframed for me how to go about looking for literary journalism topics. Sometimes I see small news tidbits in the newspaper, and I want to know more. The items are often quirky from a news standpoint yet possess what could be larger-scale, interesting themes that would resonate with many. Maybe, just maybe, there will be a story in one of these tidbits that I can someday pursue.

One of the "small news tidbits in the newspaper" I was referring to was about a pilot who had to make an emergency landing on a highway. In the brief article I read, it said he landed the small plane safely, and that thankfully no one was injured. After reading this write-up, I envisioned a literary journalism piece about this pilot getting out of bed that morning, going about his business in his usual way, taking off in the plane he flew later in the day, and then relating everything that occurred afterward. What an amazing literary journalism piece that could be!

Unfortunately, I was better at thinking about potential stories than I was at writing them. Everyone in the class was likely going through these emotions in varied ways.

It was a tough, humbling semester.

Professor Harrington often told me I was overthinking things too much at the start, and he was probably right. Sitting in as a "guest" in the usual place, Room 336, a small part of me may have thought I had a well-earned leg up on the younger students among me around the room's large table, where we critiqued each other's work. I'd been writing journalism articles for years, after all, as well as countless puff pieces for the Alumni Association and College of Education at a major research university. I certainly would wow them all—and Harrington—at some point with my literary journalism masterpiece, if I could only get the basics down first.

The course, held in the evenings, wasn't large. A past email from that period, in which the class members were all copied regarding the sharing of stories to review, shows that ten people were taking the course. Several of the students had writing backgrounds, and I sensed larger writing ambitions within some. These would be my competitors, I thought in a snarky manner, the students I'd have to impress and then blow by straightaway. Others in the class didn't strike me as having strong writing ambitions or credentials, which was comforting.

Despite the confidence I had in my past writing work, I think deep down I knew the class was going to be a struggle. These conflicting emotions may have been partly why Professor Harrington thought I was overthinking things as I wrote my articles and then received feedback around the table.

I didn't think finding engaging story topics would be as hard as it was for the first few stories. My wife, Jill, told me this task *should* be difficult—I was in graduate school, after all, and earning a master's degree was not supposed to be easy. That bucked me up a little. She suggested asking my Facebook friends what I should write about, which I did via a general post to my network of companions. What came back were several interesting ideas, a few of which I told Professor Harrington about. He rejected the topics for reasons I can't remember now, and he likely had good reasons for doing so. This was his life, after all.

One day in Harrington's office, he suggested I reach out to a former student of his, a writer who worked on campus as a communications professional and had not, like me, found literary journalism to be an easy thing to do at first. We met at a coffee shop on Green Street, where she gave me a few story ideas, one of which centered on a coming new restaurant, Watson's Shack & Rail, which was opening later in the year in downtown Champaign. I had read this news in the local newspaper and wasn't wild about covering it for my first literary journalism piece, but Harrington liked the idea. At this point I was tired of seeking out topics—and time was of the essence—so I went with it.

What followed was months of going to the restaurant, in some cases before it was even open to the public, and doing hours and hours of observational work, while also extensively interviewing the person I was focusing on, the lead cook named Mark Hartstein, better known around town as Shades. I first met him at Watson's on a bitterly cold January afternoon. The inside of the future establishment was a mess, with stuff lying around everywhere and not long to go before the joint's first soft opening. I included the atmosphere of the unopened restaurant in the first version of the story I submitted for a grade in the class. The piece was titled "Born to Cook":

Items are scattered everywhere toward the back of the restaurant, indicating much work ahead before go time. An extension cord plugged into the wall is connected to nothing. Bags, coats, and half-empty glasses dot the area. Boxes are bulkily filled with tools, caulking bottles, cables, box cutters and paint, while an unused mop and broom stand idly by. A filled-to-the-brim orange bucket has wording on its circumference that reads LET'S DO THIS, as if to help inspire everybody amid the pre-opening wreckage.

Not bad. But the problem, as I was told later during a critique of the first version of the story in class, was that this portion of the article, which occurred five days prior to a soft-opening launch that was related at the start of my piece, didn't flow well in the prose. It was solid advice, and I had to nix these pre-opening observations from all future versions of the article.

My story on Shades as lead cook and part owner of Watson's wasn't engaging Professor Harrington or my classmates like I'd hoped. Harrington had us do rewrites throughout the semester, and by my third try on this story, I'd opted for a sort of arty take on the food knowledge of Shades, relating in italics in the piece how he cooks a particular item on the menu as he works his magic in the kitchen. Here's one example from the food-making descriptions that were interspersed throughout the story:

"A little hot sauce is in there. So, then we brine that for at least six hours. It sits in this salty, kind of vinegary liquid, which promotes juiciness and a lot of moisture content and flavor that's inside the meat."

One student in the class said her eyes glazed over when she read these descriptions throughout the article. In all honesty, mine did too. It was a failed attempt to capture the creativity of cooking. My final grades from Harrington on all three of these pieces were middle-of-the-road Bs and some accompanying honest critiques in class that were hard to take. I would come home at night after classes feeling defeated. Weirdly, the last time I had felt this way was after having poor performances on the basketball court as a kid in grade school, a time in my life when I practically lived to play hoops. I'd hide these emotions from Jill as best I could, but inside, I was beginning to feel like I wasn't a real writer. Professor Harrington's guidance and the class in general felt like things that were completely separate and foreign from the knowledge I'd previously learned during my graduate school journey.

At this point I was ready to be done, but there was a long way to go to get that degree.

It was back to the drawing board as Professor Harrington and I contemplated what my next literary journalism story would be about. He told me about an African American lady his wife knew through a business she patronized. Harrington's wife said the woman—I'll call her Sheila— was in her mid-forties at the time and was personable and open. Harrington suggested the gist of the potential piece could be that Sheila was enthusiastically raising her grandson approximately eighty percent of the time, making sure he received all the support he needed. The child was in second grade and was going to enter the gifted program at his school during the next schoolyear. Professor Harrington said his wife was excited about me pursuing the story. Everything sounded promising.

I arranged to meet Sheila on a Saturday morning at her home. The idea was to get to know each other and inform her about what Professor Harrington's course was all about. I would also ask her pointed questions to learn about her background and then report back to Harrington. One important inquiry I needed answered was if she was the official guardian of the child. If she wasn't, I would have to get permission from the boy's guardian to write the story, and it was my impression that the guardian would also need to be mentioned in the article I wrote.

Sheila lived in a modest, well-kept home, and I felt at ease right away as we chatted on her couch. She was easy to talk to and indeed open about her life. I remember being surprised about the high salary Sheila said she made, though I know she worked hard running her own business. In fact, we had a limited time to talk that day since she had to go to work later.

As nice as Sheila was, the highlight of that first meeting was getting to meet her grandson. He was as cute as could be and had a shy but playful personality. The child warmed up to me the longer I was there, and I still have the pictures I took of him that day. His smile in the photos was beautiful. In the short time I was with him, I sensed something special about this kid, and I could see why his grandmother took such pride in him and wanted to raise him to the best of her ability.

After my initial meeting with Sheila, I got approval from Professor Harrington to keep going with the story. Sheila and I arranged to meet again at her house the following Saturday morning.

How different the next week was. When I arrived at her home, Sheila told me her grandson was now with his mother on a permanent basis, and that they were moving to another state. She was crying as she said these words, tears so large and authentic I could barely move and hardly knew what to say. My words of comfort sounded pathetic and useless to my own ears, and I'm sure they did little to pacify Sheila.

In a moment of utter vulnerability, Sheila told me how she had basically lived a relationship-free existence due to her son, who she said was a muscular guy with an intimidating personality that scared men off. In this way, I think she was telling me her grandson had been a source of pride and a major part of her life; with him gone, what did she have left?

Additionally, in our previous talk, Sheila had mentioned the reservations she had about her grandson being raised by his mother.

I didn't stay at her house as long that morning—there was no point in doing so. We said our goodbyes and I got in my car, feeling devastated. It was a dreary, rainy spring day. As I drove home, the thought that I might have been partly responsible for this depressing family occurrence kept popping into my head. Sheila knew I would have to get permission to write the story from one of the boy's guardians. Had she perhaps sought out this permission from her son or the boy's mother and angered one or both of them? Had that led to the mom's decision to split to another state with her son?

Perhaps I'm making myself sound too big in this episode of events, but the timing of the move always seemed strange to me. One week they were entrusting Sheila, the boy's grandmother, to practically fully raise their son; the following week, the boy's mom was making plans to leave Illinois with her son in tow. What had changed so drastically in that one-week period? Sheila seemed as baffled as me by the suddenness of the move.

I suppose I should have regarded this event as some valuable, real-world lesson that journalists must sometimes go through in a tough, unpredictable world, but that's not how I felt. I was just a graduate student trying to find an article to write, and it felt like I'd crossed a line. The situation wasn't anyone's fault, including the Harringtons, but the thought that I may have contributed to making this child's future more difficult was hard to digest.

I didn't know anything about the boy's status until emailing Professor Harrington several years later to try to get an update. Using the word "thankfully" to lead off his sentence, my old professor told me the boy was back in town and being raised by his father.

My next piece that spring semester ended up being about Urbana resident Bob Swisher, who was eighty-four years old at the time. Swisher was a well-known figure in the area for his column on antiquing that ran in *The News-Gazette*. His writing was always insightful and engaging, and I remember there was a big fuss from newspaper readers when the *Gazette* temporarily stopped publishing his articles. It didn't take long for the publication to restart Swisher's column after numerous people complained. By the time I got to know him, Swisher was no longer writing for the newspaper.

Prior to his interest and eventual expertise in antiquing, Swisher was a talented graphic designer who owned and ran his own business in town. He was also a raging alcoholic for many years, and he didn't hold back on that topic during our extensive conversations. Like Louis Postlewaite Jr. from my Immersion Journalism course, Bob Swisher was an open-book sort of guy who wanted his story to be told. He gave me an in-depth tour of his house and showed me the homebuilding projects he had worked on over the years. I also visited a storage space he rented, a large, garage-like space with loads of stuff he'd accumulated. Swisher and I also visited a few antique shops during our time together, outings that provided some moments I could incorporate into my creative nonfiction piece about him.

The critiques I got in class about the article on Swisher, as well as the subsequent rewrites I did, were comparable to the feedback I received on the piece about Shades and his restaurant. I remember Professor Harrington telling me during one class that the article about Swisher was solid. With some clean-ups here and there, it was a piece that could be published in *The News-Gazette*, he said. As Harrington related this, I noticed one of the students in class, a writer for *The Daily Illini*, was gently nodding his head in agreement. In my sullen frame of mind, I took this to be a patronizing act. The problem, Harrington said, was that what I'd written about Swisher lacked the needed components a *literary journalism* piece required. The Swisher stories got me more Bs in the class and only furthered my downtrodden outlook. By the final class, I was so dispirited that it was hard to even stay seated in the room.

At the conclusion of the semester, I said all the right things in the "What I Learned" essay I wrote about the Literary Feature Writing course. From the actual reporting and writing side of things, however, I wasn't executing the finer points of what it took to create an authentic and engaging creative nonfiction piece. That had been made clear to me by Professor Harrington and my classmates.

Harrington generously had an end-of-semester pizza party for his students in the class— I think that semester it was at Papa Del's—and that was our last hurrah as a group. My final encounter with Harrington that semester, and the last time I would see him until five years later, was in his office as he was continuing to pack things up and head into the sunset of a well-earned retirement. He told me, in a heartfelt way, that it had been his pleasure to be my graduate advisor. Going forward with the summer semester, our work together would be done remotely. I thanked him and left.

And I skipped the pizza party.

Professor Harrington brought up the term "tone poem" a few times that semester. As best I can recall, he related this style of writing as a way of concocting a different type of creative nonfiction piece, one that had a shorter word count and conveyed an overall tenor throughout. I was less interested in the "tone" aspect of this literary device than I was the abbreviated word count, which appealed to me. I thought a 1,000-word story might be just the ticket to writing something more focused and better. As the lonely summer semester began, here's how I presented my next idea to Harrington via email:

Hi, Walt -

I've been working on getting potential subjects for a story but am struggling with the commitment part of it. However, I think I can land someone soon and give you more info to see what you think.

I also have an idea for a tone poem. Every Sunday morning the C-U Second Wind Running Club gets together informally in Urbana for a jog. I'd like to participate in the next one they do and write a 1,000-word story about it. I could have all the writing gear I need and keep it in a fanny pack and hold my recorder as I jog with the group to capture dialogue. I think it would be cool to write a story in which a reader concludes that the writer jogged with everyone in order to get all the information for the story. Who knows what kind of story may emerge, but I'm inspired by the idea of writing something that feels spontaneous. I think I could do a good job with it. If you like the piece, maybe we can make it part of my final grade. If you don't like it, we can pretend it never happened. What do you think?

Thanks,
Sal

Professor Harrington gave me the go-ahead, but he told me I needed to keep working on finding a topic for a third full-length story as well. I viewed my attempt at a tone-poem type of story as a way to get "extra credit" in the class, and as a path to redeeming myself for the subpar stories I'd submitted thus far. I had a good feeling about it.

But like the attempted story on Sheila, the path veered—this time in a good way. Here is my email to Professor Harrington one week later:

Hi, Walt -

So, as you know from vast experience, stories don't always work out the way we want them to. I found that out this morning when I went to Meadowbrook Park and waited for the runners. According to the Second Wind website, they were supposed to be there at 8 a.m. I had gotten there by 7:15 a.m. just to be early and observe things.

When 8 a.m. came and went without the runners there, I noticed a group of pet owners who had Greyhounds on their leashes. I could tell immediately that they were a group who did this often, so I introduced myself, told them what I was doing and came up with an alternative story, which I've attached. I think it's a better story than anything I would have done with the runners. I didn't want to leave that park without a story, and I treated this piece as if I were on a newspaper deadline.

Interestingly, the Second Wind runners showed up at 9 a.m., right after I finished my walk with the owners of the Greyhounds. As it worked out, I was able to incorporate the runners into my story. I felt the material I collected this morning was rich enough that I could get a 1,500-word story, so that's the length I wrote instead of a tone-poem length. I hope you enjoy it.

Thanks,
Sal

Years later, I would publish this story about the Greyhounds in my book *Far From Mars*, which was a compilation of several literary journalism pieces I wrote. Here's what I wrote for the intro of the story in the book:

"Dog Devotion" was a happy accident, one of those spur-of-the-moment stories writers sometimes get lucky with. The intended piece at Meadowbrook Park was supposed to be about the members of the Second Wind Running Club, who are mentioned in the second-to-last paragraph of this story. I was at the park to meet that group prior to their running session, with the intention of jogging with them. I thought the huffing and puffing of a strenuous jog, followed by an in-depth interview or two, would make for a good literary journalism piece.

But the time on the Second Wind Running Club's website was mistakenly listed as one hour earlier than the time the group was actually meeting at Meadowbrook. I was sweating it out a bit while waiting for the runners to show up because I needed to produce a story for my final class in graduate school. No runners meant no story, and I would have to come up with another idea.

As I was waiting, I noticed all these gawky-looking dogs to my left, assembled in a group with their owners. Seeing that many Greyhounds in one spot was odd. Was this some sort of Greyhound walking group that might make for a more interesting piece than my original idea about the runners?

I didn't wait long to find out. With the bag holding my writing gear slung over my shoulder, I hurried over to the folks in the Greyhound group, introducing myself and letting them know about my writing project for school. They were fine with me tagging along on their walk.

The runners did eventually show up at the park for a six- to eight-mile jog, following my time with the dogs and their owners. Believe it or not, even after stumbling into this wonderful story about Greyhounds, I approached the Second Wind runners to see if they would be willing to work with me for a journalism piece I was doing for graduate school. They agreed and we began jogging—fast. I soon longed for the placid walk with the Greyhounds and their owners that I was just on and didn't even last a mile. I quit running and turned back to head to my car. I couldn't wait to write about the Greyhounds.

I got an A on the story from Professor Harrington, who had this to say via email:

Enterprising of you. I've been a little baffled after reading your novel at how difficult these stories have been for you. Maybe you are just over-braining them and it's making you tight.

In a subsequent email, here is what Harrington added about the Greyhound piece:

This really is nicely done. Now take this relaxed touch and apply it to a final story. I think this is publishable pretty much as is. At 1,500 words, it's probably a bit long for the N-G but you could try it there. But it really should be published locally. I'm sure Smile Politely would be interested. You really should submit it right away while it's close to the time you were there. As I said, now take this relaxed touch and apply it to your last story. I hope this cleared your head.

His words made me feel like I'd just won a Pulitzer Prize. They still have that weight today, which gives me the confidence to keep writing.

My final piece in Harrington's class was about my brother-in-law Sam Logan, who is a talented freelance photographer. On a sunny June day, we visited several locations in Champaign-Urbana as he pursued an interesting photo project. Though I wish I would have included at least a paragraph about Sam's background, I think the piece turned out well, and so did Harrington, who gave me another A and said I was now understanding the elements it took to be a literary journalist.

I was impressed with Sam's eye for detail as he photographed different buildings around town. He conveyed the importance of documenting the history of Champaign-Urbana through his photography, as well as how that could affect his own creative legacy. Sam genuinely cared about his side gig as a photographer, which was sometimes monetarily lucrative and sometimes not. In retrospect, I think his diligent efforts that day to capture specific objects through the lens of a camera influenced what I could pursue as a writer. I had done freelance writing in the past, but now that graduate school was winding down, maybe I could do it again.

Heck, maybe I could even do it on a full-time basis someday.

Chapter 7: Supporting Details

The classes discussed so far have been presented in a linear way in terms of the order I took them, but there were two courses in the program I've mostly skipped over because they didn't fit into the hard-nosed reporting and writing structure of the others. Yet the following two classes were highly influential in terms of how I came to view the process of writing a story and making sure it's as clean as can be from start to finish.

The first is the Master's Proseminar (JOUR 505) class I mentioned at the start of the book—you may recall the faded, ratty receipt from Illini Union Bookstore and the accompanying textbook titled *Mass Media Research: An Introduction*. This was the first class I took in the graduate program and the first time in seventeen years I had been in a classroom to earn a grade. The foray back into higher education was nerve-racking and exciting, but at the same time I was still in a gloomy mood over the miscarriage my wife and I had recently experienced. So, it was a difficult time.

About halfway through the Master's Proseminar course, I remember a fellow student sitting behind me saying to her classmate, "This is a weird class." I couldn't help but smile, even laugh a little inside, because I understood where she was coming from. The course was taught by Mira Sotirovic. We were in a narrow room that felt like half the size of a normal classroom, with wooden seats that climbed upward as you ascended the steps on the right side. Early in the semester, we were bombarded with external drilling and hammering noises due to construction in the building. There was a student I sat behind regularly who was very pregnant, and by late in the semester she was gone, presumably to have her baby. Another student in the course had interviewed me in the past for her class project—inquiring about my professional role in communications at the UI Alumni Association—so it was interesting, and unexpected, to reconnect with her.

But the weirdest aspect of Master's Proseminar, at least to me, was that half the time I wasn't even sure what was being covered during lectures, or what any of it had to do with journalism. It would take a while for me to fully comprehend the main concept of what was being taught, but once I understood it, the information embedded itself into my psyche and provided the foundation I needed to write future stories in the program.

My favorite memory of this class was working on a "field observation" project with my mom, who I thought might enjoy helping. The project was simple but interesting. My mom and I sat for two hours on the 600 block of Lincoln Avenue, right across the street from where I worked at the Alice Campbell Alumni Center, counting the number of people who walked, jogged, or biked past us. The goal was to determine, in a preliminary manner, if creating a biking and jogging path at this particular spot in Urbana would be a worthwhile project. "The full hypothetical biking and jogging path could potentially extend south past Kirby Avenue and end at Windsor Road, but these areas will not be observed," I wrote in my class summation. I mentioned in my report that such a path "could potentially beautify the area, possibly attracting commerce opportunities." The study encompassed "units of observation," "variables," and my pre-observation hypothesis that this would be a solid spot to have a walking path for students. The study didn't take into consideration the feasibility of widening the sidewalk to make space for a bigger path or any other aspects of construction.

Here is a portion of what we came up with while watching and recording the folks who strode past us:

In a two-hour period, we recorded a total of 207 people. Of that figure, 50.72 percent were women and 49.27 percent were men. The percentage of total walkers was 51.2; the percentage of total joggers was 6.8 percent; and the percentage of total bikers was 42 percent. The number of female walkers was 63 percent; the number of male bikers was 63 percent. The gender ratio of joggers was 57 percent male and 42 percent female. An attached contingency table (followed by the raw data) shows the modes of movement percentages by gender.

As expected, students made up the majority of people observed. It was not surprising to see so many walkers, likely because many students were coming to and from class. The same thing could be said of the bikers we witnessed, the majority of whom had backpacks on and were likely on their way to (or coming from) classes. The ratio of men and women was equal, like I expected it to be. It was a somewhat chilly day, so that may explain the low number of joggers. More joggers may have been observed deeper into the afternoon.

Overall, the healthy sample figure of 207 people observed during a two-hour period shows that a good number of students travel in this vicinity. Therefore, an exercise path could possibly be a worthwhile project. The statistics show that a high number of women walk and a high number of men ride bikes. These are both methods of movement that could take place with regularity on the hypothetical exercise path.

If we were to observe this area Monday through Friday during each semester of the school year, I am confident we would get similar statistics. I base that on the number of students who live, work, and pass through the area for entertainment purposes. By far, the biggest threat to internal validity during the course of this observation was deciphering the students and non-students on three or four occasions. There were times when this was a judgment that could have gone either way, and we did our best to make the correct decision. Throughout the study we checked with each other to verify the variables of gender, mode of movement, and student or non-student.

As stated, my theory going into this project was that the location would be a good one for a walking and biking path for U of I students. But as an unbiased journalist, I would have to test that theory (like a scientist) and be open to the fact that it *might not* be a good location for such an endeavor. A good journalist would analyze numerous factors surrounding the building of the path and interview individuals who could lend their expert insights into the project.

"Follow the evidence," Rich Martin wrote in *Living Journalism*. "Abandon your pet theory when the facts don't support it."

What this class taught me is that reporters should objectively approach their stories no different from good scientists who do thorough analyses, perform regular testing for verification, and conduct unbiased research to get their facts correct before sharing their findings to the world. This research-oriented outlook was invaluable to learn so early on in the graduate program, and I'm thankful to Professor Sotirovic for the lessons she instilled.

Another class to mention is News Editing (JOUR 420), taught by Jennifer Follis, which started in the winter of 2014, a period when I had just begun a new job in communications at the College of Education. This endeavor and starting a new class made for a stressful time.

News Editing increased my knowledge of the AP Stylebook, which I was already familiar with. It was a lab-oriented class in which we had our own computers to write headlines for scrutinizing by Follis. I have February 20 notes specifically focused on headlines that will be valuable to me for as long as I live and write. Of course, the rules of journalism change, and that includes for headlines. It seems as if it's more acceptable now to have wordier headlines, probably because of unlimited space online.

We also covered writing tasks that focused on news judgment and everyday tasks journalists perform. Follis is super sweet and an outstanding teacher. Though the work was challenging, she had a way of making it enjoyable and as stress-free as possible.

News Editing culminated with a final project in which we had to demonstrate our prowess on the multimedia part of journalism. We were encouraged to make our project professional but fun, and with a theme and images or video clips. I chose to do a blog "critiquing segments of commentary, reviews and perspectives that need a bit of editing assistance." I titled it "Opinions are Crucial for a Functioning Democracy … But Let's Clean Up the Writing, My Fellow Americans." Presentations were given on the last day of class.

My presentation in the darkened room went well, with my audience of fellow students applauding at the end, like they did for everybody's talk. I accompanied my descriptions in the project with pictures, using a blog platform I'm no longer a member of. The copy can't be found online anymore, but here was my advice, minus the hyperlinks:

Cliché: a phrase that is often used but unoriginal. An overused expression or opinion.

Example: A Feb. 24 headline in The Chronicle of Higher Education reads *Gatsby's New York State of Mind*. The phrase "New York state of mind," made popular by the song by Billy Joel, is overly prevalent in articles about New York.

The fix: Revise the headline to capture the essence of the article. In this case, the headline *Professor's book annotates Gatsby's New York era* would give readers a much better sense of what the article is about.

Inaccurate or misleading numbers in a story or graphic: Inaccurate numbers in an article could be a miscalculated percentage, the wrong square footage measurement of a location, the incorrect rebounding total for a basketball player, the inaccurate age of someone listed in an obituary, or any number of other mistakes. Misleading numbers fail to convey the most accurate or comprehensive numerical information, such as in the example below.

Example: In the Guest Commentary section of *The News-Gazette's* Sunday, Feb. 2, edition, David Bechtel noted the anti-Republican versus anti-Democrat ratio of political cartoons published by the newspaper. From August through December of 2013, he said the paper published 57 anti-liberal cartoons compared to 14 anti-conservative ones. He added that Barack Obama was featured in 44 of them, with the topic of Obamacare highlighted negatively in 34 cartoons. This disparity, Bechtel argued, disproved what a letter writer said about *The News-Gazette* printing mostly anti-Republican cartoons. I would argue that Bechtel's sample was too small, and it would be more instructive to make this sort of comparison during longer periods of time. Additionally, it makes sense that the president currently in office would have more political cartoons about him.

The fix: Show the Republican-Democrat political cartoon comparison on a year-by-year basis, and do it when presidents of opposite parties are in office. For instance, relating this comparison in 2003 (when President George Bush Jr. was in office) versus 2013 (when Obama was in office) would be more informative and accurate.

Stereotypical reference: writing that consciously or unconsciously uses language that reinforces labels, pigeonholing individuals or entities. Such writing promotes prejudice and bias.

Example: An editorial by Andres Oppenheimer about Russian President Vladimir Putin leads off with this sentence: *When Russian Defense Minister Sergei Shoigu said three weeks ago that Moscow is seeking to establish a military presence in Venezuela, Nicaragua and Cuba, many of us dismissed it as a private comment by a top official who may have had one vodka too many*. Connecting a Russian person with imbibing alcohol is a dated, overused, and mean-spirited thing to do. Alcoholism is a serious issue that should not be mentioned in jest. The last part of this sentence stereotypes Russians.

The fix: Revise the last clause of the sentence to read *many of us dismissed it as a private comment by a top official who clearly wasn't thinking straight.*

Main noun too far from the verb: when the subject of a sentence – the main noun – is separated too far away from the main verb, which can cause readers to work hard to comprehend what they're reading. This occurs when the main noun and verb are separated by clauses that might be better written as separate sentences. The clearest, most concise sentences are the ones in which the subject and verb are as close together as possible.

Example: The below lead from a story by Bruce Weber of *The New York Times* is unfortunately not opinion or commentary. It's also not the most attention-grabbing sentence, due in part to how far away the subject is from the verb. *Philip Seymour Hoffman, perhaps the most ambitious and widely admired American actor of his generation, who gave three-dimensional nuance to a wide range of sidekicks, villains and leading men on screen and embraced some of the theater's most burdensome roles on Broadway, died on Sunday at an apartment in Greenwich Village he was renting as an office.*

The fix: Rewrite the lead to say, *Philip Seymour Hoffman, perhaps one of the most ambitious and widely admired actors of his generation, died on Sunday at an apartment in Greenwich Village.*

Unnecessary passive voice: when the person or thing performing the action in a sentence does not act but is acted upon by the verb. This leads to writing that can be awkward, disconnected, dull, and irregular.

Example: Julia Bainbridge, a writer for Yahoo! Food, wrote a piece called "Remembering Jay Leno (Through Food)." Her lead has a few instances of passivity: *Last night, Jay Leno bid farewell to the "Tonight Show," which he's been hosting since 1992. Skits and cameos were made by a star-studded cast – Oprah Winfrey, Carol Burnett, Kim Kardashian, Billy Crystal, reports* The New York Times *– bringing Leno very near tears.*

The fix: This lead could be revised in a punchier way. *Longtime* Tonight Show *host Jay Leno bid farewell to the late-night world last night. Oprah Winfrey, Carol Burnett, Kim Kardashian, and Billy Crystal were by his side to make him laugh – and nearly cry at certain moments.*

Good use of parallelism and lack of parallelism: Parallel structure with words, phrases, and clauses entails using a similar pattern of words to demonstrate that multiple ideas are of equal importance. Proper parallelism in writing makes sentences sound congruent, focused, and tidy. Parallel words are grammatically balanced and pleasing to the ear. They are not choppy; they are not unequal; and they are not unrelated.

Example: A February column by John Foreman, publisher of *The News-Gazette*, revealed both good use and questionable use of parallelism in sentences. First, here is an example of consistent parallelism by Foreman in the piece: *No explanation. No rationalization. No regret.* A lack of parallelism seeps through, however, in these sentences: *There was embarrassment; there was angst; there was heartbreak; there was talk of punishment for violation of the university's code of conduct.* And this: *Caught, convicted and facing the judge who literally holds keys to the rest of their life, even the hardest cases often are awash in regret.*

The fix: The second sentence might be better written as: *Caught, convicted and about to be sentenced, even the hardest cases often are awash in regret.* Another slight misstep with parallelism in this column was apparent in this paragraph: *What did they know? Did they investigate the gaps in his resume or question why his academic credentials happened to be in someone else's name? Did they verify those credentials at all? Does the university settle for something short of vigor when hiring the army of cheap part-time instructors who make up so much of its current teaching rank?*

The fix: My suggestion would be to make the last sentence above its own paragraph, rewriting it as: *Perhaps the most crucial question: Does the university settle for something short of vigor when hiring the army of cheap part-time instructors who make up so much of its current teaching rank?*

Dangling modifier: To use the exact wording from the book *When Words Collide*: "A modifier 'dangles' when what it is supposed to modify is not part of the sentence."

Example: In the Feb. 6 edition of the *Chicago Tribune*, James Atlas wrote a piece about French President Francois Hollande visiting the U.S. Toward the end of the article, he wrote this dangling modifier: *Yet on his trip to Washington, everyone will want a glimpse of the man whom women love, who disregards social norms and does what he wants.* Obviously, "everyone" did not visit Washington if the writer is talking about a "his."

The fix: *Yet on his trip to Washington, the man who is adored by women and ignores social norms will be sought out by many.*

Inaccurate word choice: when a word in a sentence is ill-suited, incorrect, or possibly inappropriate. It is possible that adjectives, words that describe nouns, often might be the type of words that are often misused, but inaccurate word choice could occur in many instances of writing.

Example: In a February article about men's hockey in the Olympics, writer Greg Beacham used the word "perilous" to describe a future matchup featuring Russia versus Finland. He wrote: *Russia's perilous meeting with Finland is the main event today at the Bolshoy Ice Dome, where the tournament hosts will attempt to play their way into medal contention.* I see Beacham's point that this was an important game for both teams, especially Russia, but the word "perilous" makes it sound as if the Russian players were entering a life-or-death warzone, not a hockey game.

The fix: Write the first part of the sentence to say *Russia's win-or-go-home matchup with Finland* or *Russia's crucial contest with Finland.*

No news peg: A news peg is what makes an article worth writing and reading. Journalists can choose from seven well-known news values when it comes to writing stories: timeliness, impact, human interest, proximity, oddity, conflict, and prominence. If a piece doesn't have at least one of these elements, it has no news peg.

Example: A tidbit labeled "Xerox chief: Don't duplicate others' path; live your dream" in the Blue Sky Originals section of the March 10 issue of the *Chicago Tribune* is not newsworthy. Ursula M. Burns, chair and chief executive officer at Xerox, briefly shares her journey and offers worthy advice about pursuing your destiny, but the piece is not news and doesn't have a call to action. Worse yet, it says at the end to visit blueskyinnovation.com to read the full article by Burns, but the advice is no longer posted on the web page.

The fix: I'm not sure a self-help section is appropriate for a newspaper, no matter who writes it or how short the piece is. This may have been more newsworthy if Burns had related how her story correlated with running Xerox. Hearing about Burns from another writer would have perhaps made this short section feel more justified.

Misuse of a comma when the subject has compound verbs: This mistake is so common in writing that I question whether it's even a known rule in most writers' minds. A comma is not needed prior to a conjunction within a sentence when a subject has compound verbs. My feeling is that people add a comma in this spot because it feels or sounds right. The example we looked at in class was this sentence: *Superintendent Jennifer Follis said there was no doubt the school's roof needed repair but added that it might not be replaced.* No comma is needed after the word "repair."

Example: An article about McDonald's from The Associated Press had this sentence: *It blamed the harsh winter weather, but conceded that "challenging industry dynamics" also played a role.*

The fix: Delete the comma after the word "weather." The words "blamed" and "conceded" are compound verbs of the subject "It," a pronoun referring to McDonald's.

Wrong pronoun: A pronoun must match the noun it stands for (its antecedent) in number and gender. A plural pronoun such as "they" must be used when referring to a plural noun. Pronoun problems occur when using a plural pronoun such as "their" to refer to a singular noun.

Example: Writer Mike Pemberton frequently contributes to the "Voices" section of *The News-Gazette*, and in a February column he botched a few pronouns: *But in this age of "everyone can be the star of their own life" through social media, it is often a way of calling attention to ourselves; Internet mobs offer anonymity and opportunity to "overcome one's usual reticence" as no one is required to use their real name when posting.*

The fix: *But in this age of "everyone can be the star of his or her own life" through social media, it is often a way of calling attention to ourselves; Internet mobs offer anonymity and opportunity to "overcome one's usual reticence" as no one is required to use his or her real name when posting.*

Dead construction: sentences that are led off by the words "there is" and "it is." These are space-taking words that perform no function. Besides cluttering sentences, dead-construction words sap sentences of their power by transferring emphasis from what could be a strong verb to a weaker construction. To avoid dead construction, writers should not lead off sentences with linking verbs such as *is, was,* or other forms of *to be.*

Example: NBA basketball teams that "tank" (purposely lose games to get a better position in the summer draft) is the subject of a January blog post written by C. Charles (@Gilmatic). His lead to this wordy blog entry is flat and contains dead construction: *It's been a while since there's been a basketball related post on this mother* (meaning blog spot). Charles has other examples of dead construction in his write-up: *There is a rich tradition of having stupid opinions about basketball too. It's more manufactured than pop music marketed to teens. It's because professional sports are in the business of selling hope. It's their job, and in many cases, they've been in competitive situations since they were old enough to walk.*

The fix: The remedy for these sentences would be to put the verb at the forefront. *Stupid opinions abound when it comes to covering basketball. Professional sports sell hope, plain and simple. Playing hoops is what they're paid for — they've been in competitive situations since they were youngsters.*

Lack of numerical agreement between antecedents and their pronouns: when pronouns such as *it, he, she,* or *their* are not numerically parallel to the antecedents they represent. If an antecedent is singular, its pronoun must be singular also.

Example: Gene Budig and Alan Heaps wrote a column about poverty in the Feb. 2 *News-Gazette* newspaper. Deep into it, they failed to show agreement between a few words: *Giving each state the funds to develop their own program.* Two sentences later: *One, each state can tailor the programs to meet their specific needs, serving diverse populations and issues.*

The fix: Change the words *their* in each sentence to *its.* "Giving each state the funds to develop *its* own program." Interestingly, these passages read correctly in the same article online by a different publication.

Wordiness: clutter in writing; words that serve no purpose or make copy hard to comprehend. Wordy text interferes with clear and memorable passages.

Example: George Will is a smart guy, but his columns are often hard to navigate. Here's a particularly vexing sentence from a January piece by Will titled "Four words in the ACA could spell its doom": *And by enforcing the employer mandate in states that have only federal exchanges, it will collect taxes — remember, Chief Justice John Roberts saved the ACA by declaring that the penalty enforcing the mandate is really just a tax on the act of not purchasing insurance — without congressional authorization.* Whew! Will hails from Champaign, so we'll forgive him.

The fix: Delete the clause about Chief Justice John Roberts or mention it in a separate sentence.

Fact error: A factual mistake in commentary pieces, news articles, blogs, or TV newscasts could be the result of not performing proper fact-checking methods, sloppy reporting, poor editing or laziness. A common practice is to acknowledge the error and apologize for it if necessary.

Example: An editorial headline labeled "A long shot" in the April 18 edition of the paper version of *The News-Gazette* has this italicized copy underneath it: *The latest plan for expanded* *gambling in Illinois is no Christmas tree, but it would be a big gift for the Chicago.* "The Chicago" what? The word "the" should not have been included before the word "Chicago." Mistakes happen.

The fix: End the sentence by saying *a big gift for Chicago*. This part of the editorial is correct online.

I got an A on the project and escaped with an A- in the class. Throughout the semester, I noted these valuable tips from Follis:

- Language and its rules change as the years go on. A stylebook is an editor's first line of defense. Editors need a consistent method to go by, a first line of defense, especially when they're on deadlines.
- When in doubt, try to shorten the sentence. Break sentences up to analyze them. The goal is to make reading understandable.
- As an editor, always try to keep the effect the writer is striving for.
- Editing: subject, focus, order, documentation, voice.
- Breaking the rules of grammar only works when you know you're breaking them.
- Dashes are bigger pauses than commas and should only be used once per story.
- The word "which" is a pronoun; use it properly.
- When editing, make changes above the line.
- Develop a vocabulary for editing so that you know what you're talking about.
- Put the story topic in the form of a question. Helps bring focus.
- Try to coach writers all the way through. Ask writers questions so that you don't sound dictatorial.
- What do you want to know about the story and why?
- Look at the whole body of work when reviewing.
- Does the story need an alternate article for other media? Stories can get lots of mileage.
- Sometimes the strength of writing is what is left out. You can't include everything.
- Editors can sometimes be too quick to edit, just to feel useful. Let writers keep their voice. Built on a reporter's strengths. Find what works in the story. Some writers can be too comprehensive.
- "Like" is used for comparison purposes; "such as" is used for examples.
- Always look at the distance between the subject and the verb.
- Fact-check names of companies, etc.
- Understand the context of numbers in stories. You can always figure out how to compute them.
- If need be, inform the writer you're working with the stylebook you're using to justify your edits.
- A second-day lead reports on a reaction to a big story. A first-day lead tells what happened in a straightforward way. Today's media need a "second-minute" lead.
- Keep news current. If a lot of people have already heard about a story, try reporting on *why* it happened.
- Allow space for a reporter to come up with things. Ask the reporter what needs work. Never mess with copy unless you're certain.

- Read the piece first as a normal reader to get a sense of the article. Note any questions you have.
- As editors, we try to help writers improve their style. Editing is a team effort and involves making news judgements.

Afterword: The 'Why' of the Story

I received my Master of Science diploma in the mail on September 10, 2016. Jill took a picture of me holding the piece of paper and posted the image on Facebook, where it got a gazillion likes and comments.

I wish I could say the original inspiration to write this book stemmed from an idealistic desire to teach what I learned about journalism and spark an interest in others to pursue the field, which has gone through turbulent times in recent years. And though the project did evolve into me having those lofty intentions, the reality is that it was initiated by my desire to … well … simply earn some extra cash.

It all started with Rob Dial, host of the podcast *The Mindset Mentor*. One day in August of 2020, I was listening to one of Dial's shows, "How to Make Money Online." In his enthusiastic way, Dial began relating numerous money-making online endeavors, some of which, he said, raked in millions of dollars. Among other things, Dial said folks could earn good money online by posting YouTube videos, running Facebook ads for others, doing consulting work, selling supplements, setting up a Shopify store, establishing an online clothing brand, or selling other people's products via affiliate marketing.

Dial also talked about side jobs I had done in the past, tasks such as writing articles and doing freelance work for Upwork. Then he mentioned writing books for the Amazon Kindle, also something I had done before.

"I know people that make a bunch of money by finding a *specific topic*," Dial said, "and they research the hell out of that topic, and then they take that topic and put it into, like, a fifty-page Kindle book. They sell it for $4.99, but it's such a hot topic that it just goes through, and they make a ton of money doing it. So, you can literally write books in Kindle if you wanted to."

Voila. I would write about the hottest topic around—journalism—thanks to the knowledge I had amassed in graduate school, and then sit back and congratulate myself as the Amazon royalties flooded into my bank account.

I began writing, and what I found out immediately was that, while Dial's advice to churn out a profitable fifty-page Kindle read on a particular topic had its appeal, there was no way I could write such a puny book.

I simply had too much to say about journalism and those who taught it to me.

My part-time reporting days began when I was in my early thirties. That's by no means an ancient age, but it was a more advanced time frame in life than when the hardworking and passionate journalist Roger Ebert got his start. Along with Ebert, history shows a few greats in journalism got their starts in Champaign-Urbana, a town where, it turns out, writers rise. Along with Ebert, Bill Geist and George Will started their lives in C-U. My humble start in the newspaper business occurred toward the end of February 2005.

Earlier that month I'd broken up with my girlfriend on the day after Valentine's Day and, coincidentally, had a self-published novel released on the same day. You would think the latter happening would have helped ease my sorrow over the breakup, but that wasn't the case. The novel, you see, was panned by my own dear mother, who marked up her free copy with a slew of edits and recommendations following its publication, showing me in a detailed manner where I'd gone wrong. And she was right to do it, too. The book had issues and needed more polishing prior to being published. This was a few years before the onslaught of social media, so I didn't bother to promote the novel *Phantom Reunions* and let it fade into online oblivion.

It's fair to say I was feeling a little useless and down at the time.

But looking back, I recognize it was also a period in which I was anxious for something more, primed to shake things up in my life. I made a living as a copywriter and was ready to start thinking bigger, with the realization that success and attained dreams don't just fall into a person's lap. So, I answered an ad in *The News-Gazette*—one that I'd seen in the classifieds many times before—for a part-time sportswriter position at the *Mahomet Citizen*. This turned out to be a life-changing act that gave me loads of much-needed confidence.

I got the job and began working with this grizzled newspaper veteran named Bruce Yentes, who never really gave me any advice about anything, but whose demeanor helped me feel like I was an authentic fellow newspaperman. I threw myself into the part-time journalism gig, soaking in and loving every minute of the coverage I was doing. I enjoyed traveling to the sporting events to cover the games (you earned more money if you attended the events in person), and I loved talking to the coaches and players, drawing out their thoughts and formulating in my head how they might correlate with the heart of the story. I didn't love the transcribing I had to do to create the stories, but I *did* love the part that came after that: the writing. Sundays were a busy day for me as I called coaches to get their comments and then did the write-ups, waiting with anticipation afterward for the small-town newspaper to arrive in my mailbox later in the week.

Not long after I started, Yentes moved on to an editorial position at another newspaper without saying goodbye, which was kind of a bummer. I began collaborating with a much younger, cheerier editor named Michelle Robbins. As time went on my stories for the *Mahomet Citizen* evolved. Robbins was easy to work with and asked me if I wanted to start doing feature pieces, which appealed to me more than writing sports articles. This went on for more than a year, and then a few things happened that helped further the trajectory of my writing career.

The first out-of-the-blue event occurred when Emily Hills (now Emily Schmidt) called me to see if I wanted to write sports articles for a free publication in Champaign-Urbana called *The Hub*. I said yes right away, but I think I only wrote and turned in one or two sports articles during my time with that paper. The rest of my write-ups were feature pieces on various individuals in town and around the area, with one of them being a story about The Ms, a Chicago rock band I dug.

I may as well have been a journalist working for *Rolling Stone* magazine—that's how much fun I was having. The work I was doing paid little and didn't gain me any notoriety outside of my own little journalistic circle, but I was fulfilling what I felt was now a bit of a purpose in my life: telling other people's stories. I'm not sure how many people even read *The Hub* from week to week, but that didn't matter. I was doing some good work and building a portfolio.

The second unexpected happening was when Cal Acosta called me to see if I could assist with the writing of a book he was authoring titled *Remembering Robeson's*, which was about the historic Robeson's Department Store, where my dad worked for more than a decade. Similar to when Schmidt called during this period, I said yes immediately and to this day am proud to have helped with the Robeson's book project. Acosta had heard I was an aspiring writer, like him, and thought I'd be the ideal person to help with certain parts of the book. I'll always be glad he reached out to me.

One of the interviewees I was assigned by Acosta to talk to for the *Remembering Robeson's* book was a gregarious fellow named Ed Logan who, though I didn't know his daughter Jill at the time of our interview, would one day become my father-in-law. (Jill and I got married about four years later.) Ed and I chatted on the phone about his days in the mid-1960s when, as an employee of Pepsi, he would stock the Robeson's vending machines, luncheonette, and warehouse with the soft drink. Logan's efforts earned him several invitations to laid-back dinners with around ten people at the Robeson's warehouse. As I wrote in *Remembering Robeson's*, all Logan "had to bring was himself and a case of Pepsi." Others brought bottles of wine and, according to my former father-in-law, who passed away in 2013, "It was a grand time."

The Hub folded not long after I joined its staff, which was a shame because I'd stopped working at the *Mahomet Citizen* to dedicate all of my freelance writing efforts toward the former publication. But by this time, I had built up a solid repertoire of stories and was gaining confidence in my ability as a writer. I decided to reach out to *Illinois Alumni* magazine on the Illinois campus to see if that publication needed a freelance scribe, and it turned out it did. After writing a few articles at *Illinois Alumni*, where I learned more about composing stories than I ever had up to that point, thanks to editor Bea Pavia, I discovered that the Alumni Association needed a web content specialist in its communications department. I applied for the job and got it. And because Pavia knew I liked writing, she told me I could continue to pen stories for *Illinois Alumni*, which I did for the next seven years, until moving on to the College of Education.

These were good days for me; things were clicking. But I wish I'd begun my journalism career by writing for *The Sentinel* during my time at Centennial High School in Champaign. Doing so would have changed the course of my high school career and life.

Unfortunately, I didn't have the confidence to try my hand at journalistic articles as a freshman in college at Eastern Illinois University, either, due to a lack of confidence. Not committing to journalism at that time is one of my biggest regrets in life because it set me back both from a career and personal standpoint. Writing stories early on and honing those skills would have given me immeasurably improved self-assurance and steered me toward a more focused career path after college.

But I now have a master's degree in journalism, so things worked out.

A few months after earning my master's degree, I wrote a novella titled *The Newspaperman*, which I published in January of 2018. A year prior to that, I reached out to Patrick Singer at Smile Politely, who was kind enough to let me write a few literary journalism pieces for the online publication. One of them, "A Soldier of the 'Blues,'" was about a local musician named Kevin Elliott. I interviewed Elliott and afterward watched him play a show in the Great Hall of WEFT radio station. I thought the piece was one of the best I'd ever written and was one that Professor Walt Harrington would be proud of.

One of the reasons I think the Elliott article works is because the narrative contains an on-the-spot conflict and has a noticeable beginning, middle, and end to it, all good elements in longform journalism. Plus, I was able to reward readers in the end with a resolution to Elliott's predicament. Here's the first paragraph of the article:

Musician Kevin Elliott is not a blues artist, but he's going to try his hardest to sound like one tonight. Weirdly enough, his week-and-a-half-long cold that has affected his voice, and a right ear he currently can't hear out of, may assist him.

There's the conflict, right up front: this poor grizzled-sounding singer who is sick and has to get through an acoustic show that will be played live on the radio. I was able to capture in the piece some good banter between Elliott and WEFT DJ Bob Paleczny, who tries to give the singer support by telling him his cold has given him a "blues voice."

The article shifts between Elliott's live performance and general information about the musician's life. This is how I remember all of the good stories being crafted in Walt Harrington's class. Elliott was 60 years old at the time and had had an interesting life, so it's not as if the entertainment value of the story went down as I took readers away from the impending WEFT show and what happened during it by talking about the singer's past.

Complementing Elliott's concert was a whole lot of artwork being featured in the Great Hall that weekend as part of the Boneyard Arts Festival. Elliott's music, the hanging images, the tables with food and drinks all over them, and the towering shelves filled to the brim with CDs made for an arty, festive atmosphere in the small space, all of which I wrote about in the piece.

The article resolves with Elliott successfully getting through the show, with his wife joining him to sing the final song. Here's the concluding paragraph:

Elliott plays the song "Patterns of Blue," and then ends the evening with "Impressions," sung with his wife, whose melodious voice supports her husband's to the finish line. For a few minutes, under the array of rock-band names, Elliott is no longer a solo artist.

I'm not the world's most romantic guy, but I love that ending. Elliott told me later via email that he liked the article a lot, which was great to hear. In a short period of time, I'd come a long way from my despondent moments in Walt Harrington's class, when I felt as if I didn't have it in me to become a worthy literary journalism writer. Confidence is key, a must in any walk of life, and so is humility.

I'll close with this: George Will wrote a piece titled "His Neighbors Just Liked to Hear Him Talk" in the Mansion section of the September 17, 2021, edition of *The Wall Street Journal*. In it, he relates his time as a boy growing up in Champaign, calling the town "an idyllic place" in the 1950s. He wrote, "The land in Champaign was absolutely flat. There were no impediments to the horizon, no limits to how far you could travel and no obstacles to what you could do, aspirationally."

What a beautiful, metaphorical way to view the landscape of an area that most people perceive as mundane and limiting. Journalists span the world, writing important stories every day. Some of these articles entertain, and some of them spread knowledge. Journalism is not dead, and the basics of the craft can never expire.

If the news of the world and the lives within it mean something to you, learn real journalism, in all its forms. And then go out and write stories that matter.

Made in the USA
Las Vegas, NV
04 December 2022

61110427R00052